RUNNING
FOR
WOMEN
A Complete Guide

Sports Illustrated Winner's Circle Books

Sports Illustrated

RUNNING
FOR
WOMEN
A Complete Guide

by
Janet Heinonen

Photography by Warren Morgan
and Lorraine Rorke

Sports Illustrated
Winner's Circle Books
New York

Picture credits: Page 21 The Bettmann Archive, Inc.; 22 World Wide Photos; 63 (bottom) by Bill Jaspersohn; 132 by Doug Newman.

For *Sports Illustrated:* Pages 16, 162 by Manny Millan; 28 by Mike Powell/Allsport; 90 by Brian Lanker; 123 by Heinz Kluetmeier; 140 (bottom) by George Tiedemann. Cover by Carl Yarbrough. All other photos by Warren Morgan and Lorraine Rorke.

Designer: Kim Llewellyn

Library of Congress Cataloging-in-Publication Data

Heinonen, Janet, 1951–
    Sports illustrated running for women/by Janet Heinonen;
photographs by Warren Morgan and Lorraine Rorke.
        p.   cm.—(Sports illustrated winner's circle books)
    Bibliography: p.
    ISBN 0–452–26271–2
    1. Running for women. 2. Jogging. 3. Physical fitness for women.
I. Title. II. Series.
GV1061.18.W66H45   1989   89–6062
796.4′26—dc19   89 90 91 92 93 94 95 AG/HL 10 9 8 7 6 5 4 3 2 1   CIP

Contents

Acknowledgments

A special thank-you goes to Tom Heinonen, Jack Daniels, Russ Pate, Dr. Randall Lewis, Joe Henderson, Jacqueline Hansen, the University of Oregon women's track team, and the runners of Eugene for their help with *Sports Illustrated: Running for Women.*

—JANET HEINONEN
Eugene, Oregon

Introduction

Why run?

Some reasons are obvious. It's simple; it's healthy; it has also become a national pastime. If you are a woman who gave up sports when she discovered boys, lost her child's figure, or was told by her mother to "act like a lady," you will find that running is an easy and attractive way to explore the realm of athletics you may have missed because you were born female in a male-oriented sports world. On the other hand, for the current generation of girls and young women—growing up with the benefits of Title IX and the women's movement—running will be one of a myriad of sports open to them, with few strings attached.

You can dabble in running, using it strictly as a conditioner for other athletic activities. You can be more disciplined and use it to achieve the fitness you had long ago forsaken or had only dreamed about. Running can introduce you to the competitive side of your nature. You can even approach the sport with the seriousness of an Olympian and call yourself "athlete"—deservedly.

Or you can run for the fun of it. Whether you prefer solitary runs, where the mind wanders from the pressures and demands of the day, or companionable runs with friends, running can be a relaxing yet invigorating part of every day.

The ranks of women runners are growing. In the 1960s a woman was lucky to be allowed entry into a road race, luckier if there was a women's division. In the '70s she was typically outnumbered by men, 20 to 1, in a road race. Now women represent better than 25 percent of the racers and close to 50 percent of the running population. And in some races—such as the Lilac Bloomsday 12-Kilometer Run in Spokane, Washington—women racers outnumber men. A remarkable 52.8 percent of the 57,298 starters in the 1988 Bloomsday race

11

At all ages and in ever-increasing numbers, women are finding running an enjoyable and challenging sport.

These young girls, over three hundred strong, are off and running at a National Cross Country Championship.

were women. A mid-1980s study showed that the majority (57 percent) of first-year runners were women.

Women runners also have achieved near-parity in international forums. It was not until 1972 that women officially ran an Olympic race longer than 800 meters (less than a half-mile). Now they run the Olympic marathon (26.2 miles). They've also achieved paycheck parity. A generation ago women who wanted to run distances were dismissed as a "bunch of older women out for a lark." Now they're not only going the same distances as the men, they're making as much money, if not more, in the process. In 1987, for example, Portugal's Rosa Mota chalked up $73,908 in U.S. prize-money races, compared to the men's money leader, Kenyan Ibrahim Hussein ($71,800). And those figures don't include appearance fees, stipends from shoe companies, money for endorsements, or support from national governing bodies in the form of performance bonuses, expense monies, or living allowances.

From the bottom to the top of the pyramid, from millions of joggers to the handful of elite runners, women's running has truly come of age.

As for running itself, it's easy.

You don't have to be athletic to be a runner. For the woman who despairs at the thought of trying to master a passable tennis game, who trips on her feet playing racquetball, or who can't keep her balance on a bicycle, running's a snap. You may not look like Mary Decker Slaney when you start out, but the important thing is not *how* you run, it's that you *do* run.

You can approach running from any angle. Most women start running to lose weight or to become fit. Many continue running for those reasons, while others, in increasing numbers, find themselves edging into the world of competitive running. Many women "fun runners" are suddenly finding themselves at the head of the field in road races. Some, especially women with an athletic background, start running with the express purpose of competing. Others—like many men—may have run competitively at one time and find that they instinctively keep on running, whether they're competing or not.

Running is inexpensive. Outside of a good pair of shoes, you're not going to need any special equipment. Or lessons. Or facilities.

One of the joys of running is being able to step out the front door and head off on a run, unencumbered. No car to park. No equipment to deal with. No lines to stand in. No fees to pay. You're off and running free.

The world is your course. You can run around the block, at your local outdoor or indoor track, on country roads, in city parks, on mountain trails, through downtown streets, or in your high-school hallways. Some people have even measured out running courses in their backyards.

You'll find running to be a lifelong and valued friend. The relationship will at times be casual, at times intense, as you explore and relish the possibilities of the sport.

RUNNING
FOR
WOMEN
A Complete Guide

1

History of Women's Running

The article was small, a wire-service filler in the Sports Roundup section:

"BACK ON TRACK: Mary Slaney is one of the favorites in the women's division of Saturday's Mercedes Mile on New York's Fifth Avenue.

"Among those she will face in the field of 13 are Americans Kim Gallagher and Regina Jacobs, Britons Wendy Sly, Yvonne Murray and Christina Cahill, Canadians Lynn Williams and Debbie Bowker, and Elly van Hulst of the Netherlands.

"The men's field also will have 13 starters."

It was a delicious piece of irony in a newspaper which still insisted that only the bride's picture appear in the wedding section.

Moving from the society pages to the sports pages hasn't been easy for women, and even if women enjoy near-equal treatment on the playing field, there's little reflection of that fact on the sports pages. Women runners, however, have escaped the obscurity of agate type and found the big time, and along with it, big money.

A decade ago names such as Mary Decker (Slaney), Joan Benoit (Samuelson), and Grete Waitz were familiar only to the running fan. Now they're household names and worth thousands of dollars in endorsements, sponsorships, and appearance fees.

A decade ago there were no women's Olympic events longer than 1,500 meters (less than a mile).

A decade ago it took some courage and grit for a woman to start running, whether she wanted to run 1 mile or 26.

Top billing may still be infrequent, but equal billing for women runners is almost the norm. Elite and recreational runners alike can thank their forerunners for blazing the trail to respectability and recognition. As Joan Benoit

17

Joan Benoit Samuelson made running history when she won the first women's Olympic marathon in 1984.

Samuelson writes in her autobiography: "[Mary Slaney] and I didn't have to sit in or suffer the indignity of being told we couldn't possibly run with men."

LOOKING BACK

Who were those forerunners? Who were the women who defied convention and pursued the sport simply because they loved it? Who were the ones who took their cause further, fighting the political battles to gain official recognition?

Running is such a natural form of sport that thousands of women over the centuries must have shared the sentiments of Louisa May Alcott, writing of her childhood in the 1840s: "I always thought I must have been a deer or a horse in some former state, because it was such a joy to run. No boy could be my friend until I had beaten him in a race, and no girl if she refused to climb trees, leap fences, and be a tomboy."

Half a century earlier, in 1795, an English girl reportedly ran a mile in 5 minutes, 28 seconds. It would be another hundred years before a woman's footrace was fully attested and recorded. The race, over 100 yards, was added to a sports meeting near Dublin, Ireland, in 1891, and its winner was Eva Francisco in a still-respectable 13.0 seconds.

Five years later a Greek woman, running under the pseudonym of Melpomene, made the sports pages, competing unofficially in the first modern Olympic marathon. She finished the 40-kilometer race, with a bicycle escort, in 4 hours, 30 minutes. Sportswriters said that Greek officials were discourteous to refuse the lady entry and that Greek officials should be reprimanded. While Melpomene was getting all the ink, she wasn't the only woman in the race. Finishing about an hour behind her was 35-year-old Stamatia Rovithi, a mother of seven.

Women kept running races despite lack of official approval. Early in the 1900s British writers termed female runners "brazen doxies" because of their dress and habits.

By 1913 Finland's L. Aaltonen recorded a 5:44 1,500 meters. In 1918 Marie Ledru ran the French Marathon; in 1926 Violet Piercy of Great Britain ran a 3:40:22 marathon.

Rebuffed by official governing bodies, women began to form their own athletics (track and field) organizations as Europe recovered from the First World War. Alice Milliat founded the French Women's Federation in 1917 and approached the International Olympic Committee (IOC) in 1919 to add women's athletics to the 1920 Games. (Women had officially competed in the more "feminine" sports, such as figure skating, swimming, and tennis, since the 1900 Olympics.) The father of the modern Olympics, Baron de Coubertin, reacted by suggesting that all women's events be removed from the Olympics. His view was hardly surprising, considering his statement that the Olympics "must be reserved for men . . . [the] solemn and periodic exaltation of male athleticism . . . with female applause as reward."

Women's athletics were rejected again in 1924, and it took a majority vote to override IOC president Count Henri de Baillet-Latour's opposition to their inclusion in 1928. When women finally joined the Olympic track and field program, a paltry five events were offered: the 100 meters, 800 meters, 4 × 100-meter relay, high jump, and discus.

After a decade in which European and American women formed their own national federations and joined together to sponsor a women's version of the Olympics, the real thing was a comedown. If anything, the Olympic movement restricted the growth of the sport.

By 1921 seven European countries were holding women's national athletics championships. That year more than 100 women from five nations ran in an international meet in Monte Carlo, while France and England staged a dual meet which included the 1,000-meter run.

Women from France, the United States, Great Britain, Czechoslovakia, Italy, and Switzerland organized the Fédération Sportive Féminine Internationale (FSFI), which was to serve as a stimulus for women's athletics through the 1920s and '30s. The group was active until 1938, two years after the International Amateur Athletic Federation (IAAF) took control of the sport. With the FSFI's backing, Monte Carlo played host to some 300 women for a second international meet in 1922, the same year the FSFI first ratified women's world records.

The FSFI also organized a Women's Olympic Games, although they were forced to change the name to Women's World Games. Paris was the site of the first Women's Games, in 1922; Gothenburg, Sweden, was picked for the second Games, in 1926, featuring 13 events. Despite the inclusion of women's track in the Olympics, the Women's Games went on until 1934 with a much larger program than that offered in the Olympics. It was not until 1972 that the Olympic schedule equaled the number of events offered in those 1926 Games in Sweden!

Germany's Lina Radke was first to the finish line in the Olympic premier of the 800 in 1928, clocking 2:16.8 to edge Japan's Kiyune Hitomi and Sweden's Inga Gentzel by less than a second. The times were a dramatic improvement over Lucia Beard's first-recorded 800 time of 2:30.2, set in 1921.

Unfortunately, many of the Olympic competitors were scarcely fit enough to cross the finish line. Ernst Van Aaken, a pioneer among German distance coaches, saw the race and described the racers as "sprinters trying to find out whether they could finish 800 meters."

After watching unprepared women struggle through the two-lap race, the Olympic committee decreed that women should not run anything longer than 200 meters. That decision stood for 32 years. Not until the 1960 Games in Rome were women allowed to compete in the 800 again, and only in 1972 was the 1,500 added. It would take a revolution in women's running, legal battles, and intense politicking to give women distance runners a measure of parity in the Olympics, with the inclusion of the 3,000 and marathon in 1984 and the 10,000 in 1988.

While women's distance races on the track stagnated for half a century, other forms of the sport were hardly thriving. Only the Scots, Welsh, and English offered cross-country and road racing for women from 1920 through the 1940s. Meanwhile, in the United States road runners organized in 1957 to promote their sport and encouraged race directors to let women compete, even if unofficially.

The first nationally recognized cross-country race (1½ miles) in the United States, run around Seattle's Green Lake in 1965, was won by a teenager named Marie Mulder, usually a half-miler. It wasn't until 1971 that a woman's time for 3 miles on the track was officially recorded (17:07 by Cheryl Bridges of the United States).

Longtime women's track coach and former U.S. Olympic coach Ken Foreman bemoaned the lack of progress in this sport for women, pointing out that few advances had been made since the Greeks beheaded any female who dared to watch a warrior athlete perform. He cited the example of the superintendent of schools who refused to let girls run cross-country because they would just go into the woods with the boys. That attitude was reinforced in the courts by people such as Judge John Clark, who ruled in 1973 against a Connecticut girl who wanted to run on her school's cross-country team. Noted Judge Clark: "Athletic competition builds character in our boys. We do not need that kind of character in our girls."

And so went the world of women's distance running, moving a step backward for every two steps gained. Then along came a fitness boom, the jogging craze, and the women's rights movement.

In the early 1960s President John Kennedy roused the American public to pursue physical fitness. About the same time, Bill Bowerman, University of Oregon track coach, returned from a trip to New Zealand, where distance

The start of the first Olympic 800-meter for women in 1928. Many competitors, unprepared for the distance, struggled to finish, and the Olympic Committee didn't allow women to race over 200 meters again until the 1960 games.

coach Arthur Lydiard had introduced him to the benefits of jogging. Bowerman and Dr. W. E. Harris began research into the effects of jogging and developed a jogging program for individuals, from the sedentary to the moderately active. When they published a book called *Jogging,* the gospel was spread.

Dr. Ken Cooper expanded the principles of jogging into a broad-based fitness program which he detailed in his book *Aerobics.* Thousands of American men and women embarked upon fitness programs for the first time in their adult lives. For many, jogging became the principal form of exercise.

Although not all fitness buffs stayed with their programs, many did, even past the point where fitness was their sole goal. The competitive instinct stirred. For men, the logical extension of fitness running was competitive running in long-distance races, previously the solitary, sweaty domain of the marathoner.

Women took a bit longer to crash into that so-called lonely world. After all, most women had never before competed athletically, and society had encouragement and adulation only for those young enough to have a chance at the Olympic gold. Certainly the image of middle-aged women plodding along at an 8-minute-mile pace would never catch the fancy of the American public. Little did they know.

Breaking into the headlines in 1967 came Katherine Switzer, a 20-year-old journalism student, who entered the males-only world-famous Boston Marathon. When race director Jock Semple discovered a woman hidden beneath the ample sweat clothes, he attempted to physically remove her from the field. Photos of his efforts appeared in newspapers across the country—the feisty little Scot trying to yank the young coed off the street. Switzer's massively built boyfriend stepped into the fight, and Switzer continued on her way, finishing the race in 4 hours, 20 minutes. Ironically, Switzer wasn't the first woman to cross the finish line at Boston that year. Roberta Gibb Bingay, who had run unnoticed in 1966, finished in an unofficial time of 3 hours, 40 minutes—well ahead of Switzer.

Eight years later Switzer cruised across the same finish line in 2 hours, 51 minutes, a time which would have won the first Boston Marathon (1897). Switzer's finish caused little stir this time because she was entered with Semple's blessings, and another woman, West Germany's Liane Winter, had already beaten her to the finish line, setting a women's world record of 2 hours, 42 minutes, 42 seconds—well ahead of some 1,500 runners in the field of more than 1,800 finishers.

In 1967 Kathy Switzer opened a new world of distance running for women as the first female to run officially in the Boston Marathon.

Men and women run side by side in most of today's distance events.

What had changed in those eight years?

As the women's rights movement gained steam in the early 1970s, along with it came Title IX of the 1972 U.S. Education Amendments, which forbid sex discrimination in institutions using federal funds. Title IX opened a new world of opportunity for women student-athletes, from grade school through college. By law, women's sports had to be provided in schools.

But women were still prohibited from competing in races longer than 2½ miles. In 1970 a group of women, many of whom had started as fitness runners, approached the Amateur Athletic Union (AAU) to gain official sanction of long-distance running for women, but the AAU's committee for women's track and field dismissed the idea, calling it a "lark."

Sanctioned or not, women ran in men's races. In many cases they were warmly welcomed by race officials and were occasionally allowed to compete in their own women's division. At other races officials were unprepared for female competitors, so the women simply signed up in the men's open division and kept on running.

In places where AAU sanctions were more strictly felt, trouble brewed. At the 1972 New York City Marathon, women were told that they would have to start 10 minutes before the men. When the gun fired, six women sat down on the starting line. They finally started when the official gun sounded, but their times were never adjusted. Race directors in Tigard, Oregon, tried the same tactic in an 8-mile road race. This time the women grumbled but agreed. Caroline Walker, a diminutive teenager from Portland, sped off and arrived at the finish line before the officials. The next year both sexes started from a common gun.

The AAU eased its stand in November 1972, ruling that men and women could start the races together, as they had earlier that year in the Boston Marathon, with Jock Semple's blessing. As Semple himself put it, "Respectability is what counts," and women runners were now respectable.

Women's long-distance running eventually split from AAU women's track and field, and in 1974 the AAU sponsored the first women's national marathon championship.

As the swell of recreational runners pushed the sport ahead, the pioneers of the elite were already producing times to show that women could handle the demands at the top.

Doris Brown (Heritage), Foreman's star pupil, was running 100 miles a week in 1966. Her track career had started in 1958, when 200 meters was the longest Olympic event. Brown won the first of five world cross-country titles in 1967 in a meet which U.S. women—not men—dominated, but with virtually no recognition. She set a world record of 4:41.4 for the mile that year, opening the gates for runners such as Francie Larrieu (Smith), who raced with men as a 13-year-old in '67, ran the metric equivalent of a 4:25 mile a decade later, and came within a second of the American record in the final of the first Olympic women's 10,000 in 1988. Watching that race in Seoul was Heritage, who had coached U.S. women distance runners in the 1984 Olympics and was recently elected to the IAAF's cross-country and road-race committee.

Heritage and others had been on the opposite side of the fence a few years earlier, when the IAAF and the IOC drew battle lines to stymie the addition of women's distance events to the international program. The IAAF was generally favorable to the idea but did not put full pressure on the IOC to accept new events. Instead, the pressure came from outside groups, led by runners and coaches.

Ernst Van Aaken organized the first international marathon for women, held in 1974, in Waldniel, West Germany. The Avon corporation, with Switzer leading the way, picked up sponsorship of the marathon in 1978, when the race was run in Atlanta, the first time in the U.S. Avon expanded the program to an International Running Circuit for Women that grew to 50 races in 19 countries.

The 1978 Avon Marathon was the first international women's marathon held in the United States. One hundred eighty women competed in the 26.2-mile event. The winner was Marty Cooksey, with a time of 2 hours, 46 minutes.

In the meantime, official acceptance of women's distance running was seeping up from the scholastic levels, thanks to Title IX. Now boys and girls both regularly run 3,000 meters (or a near equivalent) in their high-school track meets. On the collegiate level, men and women have almost identical running events, with the flat 3,000 for women replacing the 3,000-meter steeplechase for men. College women, then under the leadership of the Association for Intercollegiate Athletics for Women, added the 10,000 to its championship program in 1979, nine years ahead of the IOC. (The men's National Collegiate Athletic Association took over women's collegiate sports in 1981–82, holding coed championships for the first time in cross-country and track.)

Olympic officials continued to dig in their heels on the issue of women's distance running, ignoring performances such as Grete Waitz's startling 2:32:30 debut in the New York City Marathon in 1978 (followed by 2:27:33 in

1979 and 2:25:42 in 1980). The officials' view ignored the fact that no man broke 2:26 until 1947, or that Waitz's 1980 time was fast enough to earn a medal in each of the men's Olympic marathons through 1956. It also ignored the fact that the Norwegian runner beat a field of 1,780 *women* in the 1979 race.

Dismayed at the IOC's inaction, an international group of concerned runners including Heritage, writer Joe Henderson, and Jacqueline Hansen (the first woman to break 2:40 in the marathon) formed the International Runner's Committee (IRC) in 1979 to lobby for women's distance races and other runner-related issues.

With financial backing from Nike shoe company and individual donations, the IRC took its case to the IAAF and the IOC. The committee gained support from IAAF president Adriaan Paulen, who in 1979 promised to boost efforts to include the 5,000, 10,000, and marathon in the international program. Twentieth Century Fox, a major backer of the Los Angeles Olympics, sponsored a Women's International Marathon on the course to be used in the 1984 Olympics. Senator Nancy Landon Kassebaum (Kansas) introduced a resolution in support of parity for women runners in the Olympics. The American College of Sports Medicine issued a statement saying that women should not be denied the opportunity to compete in long-distance running.

In the spring of 1980, Switzer, with Avon's backing, presented the IAAF with a status report on the growth of women's running. At that time 20 countries had national marathon records of 2:55 or faster. Waitz's current world record of 2:27 would have won all the Olympic marathons before 1952.

And women kept on running. Joan Benoit began to close the gap on Waitz in the marathon. The 3,000 and marathon were added to the women's events for the 1982 European Championships and the 1983 inaugural World (IAAF) Championships. The 1980 U.S. Olympic Track and Field Trials held women's exhibition races at 5,000 and 10,000 meters. The 1980 Avon International Marathon in London was televised worldwide by BBC and NBC. Waitz ran 31:00 to best a field of 4,600 women in the L'eggs Mini-Marathon 10,000-meter road race. In 1982 the IAAF finally recognized world records for women at 5,000 and 10,000 meters.

At Moscow in 1980 the IOC finally approved the 3,000 for inclusion in the 1984 Games, but continued to waffle on the marathon. At issue were an initial reluctance on the part of Los Angeles organizers to add any events, reaction to the U.S.–led boycott of the 1980 Olympics, the "need for more medico-scientific research and experience," and the IOC's rules on the process for adding new events.

Heeding the urging of Paulen, the IOC agreed to keep the issue alive, and at its next meeting, in early 1981, finally gave approval to the marathon, bending its own rules to do so, a not-unheard-of occurrence.

Progress, definitely. Parity, not yet.

The IRC, grateful for the action on the marathon, continued to lobby hard for the 5,000 and 10,000—events to fill the gap between 3 and 42 kilometers. Ilse Bechtold, of the IAAF's Women's Committee, encouraged the federation to explore those events for future inclusion.

In the summer of 1982, the IRC sent a letter to Bechtold under the signatures of the three latest world-record holders in the 5,000—Paula Fudge (Great Britain), Anne Audain (New Zealand), and Mary Decker (U.S.)—asking for the inclusion of the 5,000- and 10,000-meter events in Los Angeles. The IAAF responded by awarding a 10,000 to the 1987 World Championships and a world road 10,000-meter championship in 1983. The 5,000 was not considered.

Represented by the American Civil Liberties Union, the IRC filed a last-ditch suit against the IOC in 1983, seeking the addition of the 5,000 and 10,000 to the 1984 Olympics. Some 50 elite women runners from 20 countries, including Decker, Waitz, Rosa Mota, and Lisa Martin, were listed as plaintiffs. The suit was announced to the world press as many of those women gathered for the first World Track and Field Championships in Helsinki. Fittingly, it was Waitz, the pioneer, who won that first officially sanctioned world championship marathon. And it was Decker who elevated world consciousness of women's running by her thrilling and gutsy to-the-wire victories in the 1,500 and 3,000.

U.S. District Court Judge David Kenyon rejected the sex discrimination suit; however, he acknowledged that there was a "male-oriented approach taken in the Olympics" and that "there must be a great frustration for a woman athlete with the talent and determination to be the best and who, had she been a man, could compete in [the 5,000 and 10,000]." A federal appeals court upheld the ruling, 2 to 1. Dissenting Judge Harry Pregerson said that the IOC had violated California civil rights laws and that as a result, "the Olympic flame . . . will burn less brightly."

A month later the IOC approved the 10,000 for the 1988 Olympics, even before the IAAF made a formal request.

The 5,000 remained an orphan event.

WELCOME TO THE BIG TIME

As the political battles raged in the background, women's distance running truly achieved legitimacy in the 1980s. Distance running went professional, and

Florence Giffith-Joyner amazed the track world by winning three gold medals and one silver at the 1988 summer Olympics, where she also set a world record in the 200-meter dash (21.34 seconds).

women runners with it. Prize money, trust funds, certified courses, improved record-keeping, appearance fees, road-racing circuits, Grand Prix track circuits, worldwide publicity, and mega-races affected men and women on a mostly equal basis. And with the pluses came the minuses: the use of illegal drugs to gain competitive advantage; blood doping; unscrupulous coaches, managers, and agents; runners who cheated; and the hard-to-resist temptation to sacrifice quality training and racing in order to make quick cash on the roads.

The 1984 Olympics personalized women runners for the public. Home-spun Joan Benoit's courageous run in the Olympic Trials 17 days after knee surgery and her stunning win in the first Olympic marathon for women made her a heroine. Mary Decker, who had been setting fire to the record books, and the ill-fated South African cum Briton Zola Budd tangled feet in the first women's Olympic 3,000. Decker's fall left a lasting image and kept alive interest in the event long after the Olympic torch was extinguished.

Another pair of track women—sisters-in-law Florence Griffith-Joyner and Jackie Joyner-Kersee—captured the gold and the limelight in the 1988 Games. Griffith-Joyner, in particular, confounded the track world with sprint times equaling those of the legendary Jesse Owens, and more recently, O.J. Simpson. Although not distance runners, the pair's successes (five gold medals between them) and ensuing recognition proved that women were indeed accepted as bona fide competitors, not as a sideshow to the main event. In fact, watching Olga Bondarenko of the Soviet Union gun down Great Britain's Liz McColgan in the 10,000, and Rosa Mota surge in the final kilometers to win the marathon, it was hard to imagine that those events in Seoul hadn't been part of the Olympic program for years.

RUNNING AND THE MARKETPLACE

Numbers in women-only races have grown impressively over the past decade, despite a recent cutback by race sponsors in general. The Alaska Women's Run went from 257 runners in 1979 to 2,935 in 1988. The Stockholm Tjejmilen 10.3-kilometer run drew 1,600 women in 1984 and 24,000 four years later. The Dublin Women's 10-Kilometer also boasts five-figure fields, with 14,000 running in 1988. There are, however, fewer all-women's races being offered as sponsorship dollars become more scarce.

L'eggs narrowed its commitment to one annual event, New York City's mini-marathon, the nation's largest women's race. Bonne Bell, one of the leaders in women's race sponsorship, backed 26 races in 1979 but only 6 in 1986. The Avon Running Circuit was discontinued entirely in 1984, again due to the economic factors that caused many race sponsors to cut back or curtail their involvement with the sport. Road-race directors are meeting more competition for the sponsor's dollar—from sports such as triathlons, swimming, cycling, biathlons, and cross-country skiing. Many of the participants in those sports got their start as runners.

2

Beginning Running

The old cliché about the first step being the hardest is certainly true when it comes to running. Getting started is the most difficult step. Yet common sense, a schedule, and a personal commitment are all you'll need in the beginning. Once hooked, you will make running as much a part of your daily ritual as eating or sleeping.

THE FIRST STEPS

If you haven't actively engaged in athletics for a long time, your first step is to take a serious look at yourself and to evaluate your state of health and fitness.

Chances are good that you're overweight, since weight control is what frequently starts women running. An average woman's body is composed of 25 percent body fat, but most women runners measure in around 15 percent, just about the same percentage as that of the average male. Most women don't have access to skin-fold calipers or underwater weighing systems to accurately determine body-fat percentage, but a full-length mirror and a quick pinch at the waistline will give you a pretty fair indication of a weight problem.

Slim women are going to have an easier time starting off. An overweight woman should take her program more slowly, but if she can cut back at least minimally on her caloric intake, she soon should see some changes in that mirror image.

The Importance of a Physical

If you lead a sedentary life (and are out of breath after one flight of stairs), it's important to have a physical exam before starting any kind of exercise program.

Beginning runners, like their more advanced counterparts, should train, not strain. When starting out, take your running slow and easy.

Even if you are active and feel in perfect health, a physical is still a good precautionary measure and may turn up some information that will be important as you pursue a training program.

In *Aerobics for Women,* Mildred Cooper lists several factors that may rule out running or jogging. If you're more than 35 pounds overweight, you should first lose weight on a walking program. You should not consider jogging if you have heart disease, and heart attack victims should wait at least three months before starting a jogging program, doing so then only under strict medical supervision.

Severe heartbeat irregularities calling for medication or frequent medical visits may preclude jogging, as do uncontrolled sugar diabetes and uncontrolled high blood pressure. Persons with these problems should not run without their doctor's permission. (Doctors may recommend running in such cases; running helps some individuals reduce their need for medication.)

Other conditions will allow jogging, but only under medical supervision. In this category, Cooper includes infectious diseases in the convalescent or chronic stage; sugar diabetes controlled by insulin; internal bleeding; anemia; lung disease that causes difficulty in breathing, even with light exercise; high blood pressure that can be reduced only to 150/90 with medication; blood-vessel disease of the legs which causes pain while walking; arthritis; and convulsive diseases not completely controlled by medication.

Obviously, someone suffering from any of these problems is already likely to be under a doctor's care, but it is important to realize that even severe medical problems may not stand in your way. In fact, your condition may be helped by running. Scores of heart attack victims who have recovered and gone on to complete marathons will attest to the regenerative powers of running.

Keep a Notebook

Once you have medical clearance, it's worthwhile to start a notebook in which you write down the results of weekly weigh-ins, periodic checks with the measuring tape, workouts and reactions to workouts, race results, and notes on illness and injury. By keeping a log, you can easily measure your progress in terms of distance, speed, consistency, weight and inches lost, and attitudes about running. In the case of injury, you may even be able to look back and pinpoint the predisposing factors.

After you've checked with your doctor, all you need is a good pair of running shoes and some comfortable clothing (see Chapter 3), and you're ready to go.

Keeping a notebook is a good way to monitor your progress as a runner. In it, you can log distances run, times, any ailments you might have, even your mood.

GETTING STARTED

It is best to start your program as part of a group, forcing yourself to make a commitment and to set aside certain hours each week for running. If you're a student, you've got a variety of options. Your school probably offers a jog-run or fitness class, as well as a track and cross-country team. University jogging classes are often open to the public, as are jogging programs sponsored by local YMCAs, park and recreation districts, and other organizations. Younger runners should also look into local track clubs that offer coaching and competition for girls. Older runners may discover running or track clubs in their areas which sponsor social runs on a regular basis. In Great Britain a popular "Sisters' Network" pairs "Big Sisters" (veteran runners) with "Little Sisters" (novice runners) to help the neophytes get started. Since the program began in 1983, the percentage of women participating in road races there has doubled.

Personal coaches, virtually unheard-of a few years ago, with the exception of those coaching elite runners, are starting to crop up. For a fee, a running coach will provide personalized workouts and advice, and probably help match you with runners of similar abilities. Such coaches may have a fitness consulting business, work for a sports medicine center, or operate informally. Most are reputable, but given that anyone can hang out a shingle, be wary of the running-as-religion, coach-as-guru approach. Don't be afraid to ask around about personal coaches. Word-of-mouth recommendations and evaluations are important. Talk to other runners or talk to established high-school or college coaches in your area before you put your money down for a personal coach. Although personal coaches are ostensibly in business to help you run faster, many of the people who take advantage of those services say that the group experience is the main attraction. Whether or not they set any PRs (personal records), the runners enjoy immensely the chance to train as a group, partly for the "push" that others can provide in training, but mostly for the camaraderie.

If no programs exist where you live, or if you can't fit one into your schedule, enlist a friend to start running with you. Your biggest problem will be finding a companion of similar fitness so that your running doesn't develop into a challenge race every day. If you have a nine-to-five job, talk your employer into an extra 30 minutes at lunchtime and get a running group organized. You'll come back from your break invigorated and alert, while the nonrunners fight postlunch drowsiness.

Male runners often encourage their wives, girlfriends, sisters, or mothers to start running. The encouragement is great, but don't feel obligated to go for a run with your male friend or relative unless you're sure that you'll both be comfortable at the same pace. Your first weeks of running are likely to be more perspirational than inspirational, and having a companion running circles around you can be exasperating.

Whether you're running alone or with others, try to set a regular time for your workout. Studies have shown that individuals who run in the mornings before starting their daily routines are more likely to stick with their programs. If you're a late-afternoon runner, it's easy for things to come up and get in the way, unless you're willing to schedule your running as you would a business appointment.

School track teams and local running clubs offer coaching and regular competition to the aspiring runner. It's easier to do your fast-pace running with a group.

Human and canine companionship can help make your running what it should be—safe, healthy, and fun.

RUNNING SAFELY

Your single most important safety measure may be a running partner—human or canine.

Women runners—especially solitary ones—are, unfortunately, an easy target. For all the freedom that running offers us, the fear of harassment and assault confines and limits our ability to fully realize that freedom. RunHers, a Washington, D.C., running group, surveyed 100 women runners and found that 46 had been threatened by men. Incidents ranged from pinching and indecent exposure to direct physical attack. The women also reported 44 threats from car drivers, 16 from bicyclists, 79 from dogs, and 20 incidents of objects thrown from vehicles.

The group offers the following safety tips:

• Avoid unpopulated areas such as parks, bike trails, and deserted tracks and streets.
• Carry a whistle or air horn (available at bike shops). Air horns are useful against men and dogs.
• Notice who is ahead of and behind you and where the nearest people or populated areas are.
• Follow your intuition. If an area seems suspicious, turn back.
• Tell someone where you are running. Identify your favorite routes to a friend, or write down where you plan to run.
• Run in familiar areas.
• Think about possible escape routes in case of an attack.
• Run with a partner or a large dog whenever possible.
• Run widely around places where men might hide, such as parked vans, trucks, bushes.
• Ignore verbal harassment.
• Use discretion in acknowledging strangers.
• Carry money for a telephone call.
• Carry an I.D.
• Leave entertainment devices, such as a headset or radio, at home. Wearing such devices, you cannot hear people, vehicles, or dogs coming up behind you.

An obedient dog (and one who can run your pace) is an excellent deterrent to would-be attackers. Project Safe Run, of Eugene, Oregon, rents dogs to runners and trains dogs to protect their owners. Safe Run director Shelley Reecher trains dogs for defense only, not as attack animals. Even an untrained

She started her program out of frustration. "I just got sick of being hassled," she recalled. "I had people pinching me on my rear end, people running by, making personal remarks, then streaking off when they knew I couldn't catch them." With a lifelong background in animal training, Reecher used her experience to train her own Doberman for personal protection.

"Now, when I run with the dogs, the comments are so generic, like 'Nice dog you got there' or 'Nice day for running.' If I don't have to get upset about some jerk, my run is that much more enjoyable."

While your own dog may provide protection, strange dogs may pose threats. Your best line of defense is to avoid the dog: get out of his territory, even if it means crossing the street. If you feel you are in imminent danger, you can throw gravel, stones, or dirt clods to scare it away.

A final safety note: If you must run when it's dark, wear reflective clothing. Many shoes are now equipped with reflective striping; likewise many running jackets. You can buy inexpensive reflective vests or reflective tape to attach to your clothing. On dark, rainy nights, foggy days, during early morning hours, or at dusk, it's almost impossible for a motorist to see you if you're not wearing reflective material.

THE TRAIN, DON'T STRAIN, AND HARD/EASY PRINCIPLES

After you take stock of your physical condition, treat yourself to a good pair of running shoes, locate a running site, and make the commitment to give running a try, you're only a step away from being a runner.

Commit to memory two basic precepts set forth by Bill Bowerman in *Jogging:* "Train, don't strain," and the "hard/easy principle."

If you've taken 10 or 20 or 30 years to get out of shape, don't expect to reverse the process overnight. You've got the rest of your life to get in shape and stay in shape. You can recapture a high degree of fitness, but it will take time. Your object is to train your body without straining it. As a beginner, your goal should be to finish a workout exhilarated, not exhausted.

Almost without exception, joggers begin by running too fast. Your first steps may be nothing more than a slow shuffle or even a fast walk. Use the "talk test" to find your proper running pace. If you can't talk while running, you're running too fast. Slow down.

Alternate jogging and walking is the best way to start a running program.

The hard/easy principle can be applied to all levels of running, from the 3-miles-a-week jogger to the Olympian training for her dream race.

It is based on the idea that for every period of hard work you must rest, and that the harder you work the greater your need for rest. Runners progress more rapidly and painlessly by alternating hard work one day with easy work the next. The body needs a chance to regenerate itself after the stress of exercising, and the rest or easy days in your program will help you avoid chronic states of fatigue.

The hard/easy principle also helps ensure moderation, so important in the application of gradual stress to your running. As Bowerman points out, someone who can run a mile in only 7 minutes does not prepare for a 5-minute mile

by trying to run one every day. Instead, the wise runner gradually approaches
her goal, bit by bit, day by day, week by week, and year by year. Don't hesitate to set goals, but keep them realistic and be aware that intermediate goals must be met along the way.

Keep your running structured but creative. Approach it with a plan that enforces regularity but allows you to experiment in a variety of ways, from changing your running sites and times to including test runs and runs at varying paces. Variety will keep your sport from becoming stale, and a plan will help you enforce the hard/easy and train, don't strain principles.

Running is a sport that demands commitment. You have to stick with it to achieve results—whether they are weight loss, faster times, or simply a sense of well-being. As Mildred Cooper writes, your running can be the one area of your life where you have discipline: "No matter what else happened during the day, I can say to myself, 'Well, I got my exercise in.'"

YOUR TRAINING PROGRAM

The best program for the beginning jogger includes alternate jogging and walking. A very unfit person or an older person should first consider walking, working up to 30 minutes at a brisk pace, before embarking on a program of alternate walking and jogging.

As a beginning jogger, outline for yourself a five- or six-day-a-week program; each hard day's mileage need not exceed half a mile for those who are quite out of shape or 1 mile if you are more fit. An easy day (on alternate days) should include some formal exercise, even if it is just walking.

Each hard-day session should begin with 2 or 3 minutes of walking and some stretching exercises, to get your muscles warmed up. Stretching exercises should always be slow and deliberate rather than quick, lunging, or bouncy. Specific areas that need stretching include the Achilles tendons, the calf muscles, the hamstring muscles (at the back of your thighs), and the quadriceps (at the front of your thighs). Running tends to tighten and shorten the muscles in your legs, so stretching those muscles regularly is necessary to maintain flexibility. You can also add some upper-body flexibility exercises to your warm-up routine. These exercises will improve mobility in the upper body and help you run with a more relaxed carriage. (See Chapter 6 for specific exercises.)

The "talk test"—being able to talk to a companion while running—is a good way to ensure that you are running at a reasonable pace.

The Workout

Depending on your level of fitness, you will probably need to break the total workout distance into segments, alternating walking with jogging. For example, your first hard-day workouts might look like this:

Warm up (walking, stretching).
Jog 55 yards. Walk 55 yards. Repeat four times.
Jog 110 yards. Walk 110 yards. Repeat four times.
Jog 55 yards. Walk 55 yards. Repeat twice.
Warm down (walk until you feel recovered).

You may find it easiest to begin your program at a track where each lap is 440 yards, with four laps equaling 1 mile (newer tracks will probably be 400 meters in length, about three yards short of a quarter-mile). Many communities also offer jogging trails with various distances marked off. If a track or trail isn't convenient, you can try running with a watch, alternating a minute of running with a minute of walking and so forth. The point is, don't try to run the whole distance at once. But do try to finish it, even if you have to walk much of it.

When you feel comfortable covering the 1-mile distance in a workout, you can gradually start to increase your mileage—not your speed—and cut down on the amount of walking between running intervals.

Your easy days should be programmed for activity so that daily exercise becomes a habit. Set aside time for a light jog, a walk, a bike ride, a swim, or exercises, but be regular.

Your weekly hard/easy schedule would probably look like this:

Monday: Hard
Tuesday: Easy
Wednesday: Hard
Thursday: Easy
Friday: Hard
Saturday: Easy
Sunday: Rest

You may be able to run a nonstop mile in your second or third week of training and, after six weeks, be up to 2 or 3 miles a session. You should see your first big improvement in fitness by the end of 10 weeks.

LSD Running

After two months or more, you can try to jog the entire distance of your workout. Go slowly and avoid overstressing your body. If you can comfortably handle the distance, you're ready to embark on what is termed long slow distance running, LSD for short.

At this juncture many women will want to stabilize their programs, being content to maintain a good fitness base. Their programs should include three to four days of jogging a week, on alternate days. Total distance logged can vary from 2 to 5 miles per session.

But if you are interested in some form of competitive running, you will need to increase your mileage to a minimum of 20 to 25 miles per week before racing. Anyone considering races of up to 10 miles should be running a mini-

A number of communities now provide jogging trails with exercise stations spotted along the way. At each stop, the runner can perform a different strength exercise, all of which, combined with the aerobic activity of running, provide an outstanding total conditioning program.

mum of 30 to 35 miles per week. Longer races call for a base of 40 to 50 miles a week or more.

It's important for a woman runner with no previous running experience to build a solid base of LSD running before attempting to develop speed. Interval training (as outlined in Chapter 7) can produce quick results for unfit teenagers, but the runner quickly plateaus and never makes the kind of progress she would have if she had first built a solid base of aerobic fitness.

The 1-Hour Run

You should be able to run for an hour (6 to 8 miles) without much discomfort before trying any type of fast running. To reach this point, try to run daily, or six times a week, again relying on the hard/easy principle.

The week you attempt your first 1-hour run might look something like this:

Day 1 (easy): 15 to 20 minutes running (2 miles)
Day 2 (hard): 35 to 45 minutes running (4 to 5 miles)
Day 3 (easy): 15 to 20 minutes running (2 miles)
Day 4 (hard): 35 to 45 minutes running (4 to 5 miles)
Day 5 (easy): Rest or 10 to 20 minutes running (1 to 2 miles)
Day 6 (hard): 1-hour run
Day 7 (easy): 15 to 20 minutes running (2 miles) or rest

Some women can easily manage an hour's run after a few months of jogging. Others may take several years to reach that point. No matter. Go at your own pace.

As you attempt to meet the 1-hour-run goal, you may want a regular time trial (timed run) to gauge your improvement and give you an early idea of pacing, important if you decide to do speed training and compete. Time yourself for a mile on a track once every two to four weeks, running comfortably but still faster than during a normal workout. Note your time at the end of each lap so that you can see if you are running an even pace. If you ran a mile in 8:00 at an even pace, each lap would take 2:00. An even pace is important because it's more efficient. Make it your goal.

Fun Runs

If you feel comfortable with someone timing you, you may want to try a fun run.

Varying from 1 to 10 kilometers (less than 1 mile to 6.2 miles), fun runs are informal road races held just about anywhere running has become popular. Low-key, they give you a chance to test yourself off the track, running with others on a measured course, which, you'll discover, makes your efforts easier. Many fun runs are held regularly at the same site, so you can measure your progress. Others many be held annually, or as auxiliary races at longer events.

Increasing Mileage

The best way to increase mileage as you train for longer runs is to do so gradually. Too many women, their enthusiasm high, jump into a 10-miles-a-day program, although their previous training averaged only 5 or 6 miles. The results are usually predictable: stress injuries and fatigue. These women have ignored the hard/easy principle.

Easy days should be kept constant—you might run only 2 to 5 miles on your easy days while slowly building up your mileage on hard days, once a week adding an extra mile or two to your long-run day.

Here is a typical week's training program as you slowly increase your weekly mileage:

Day 1 (easy): 2 to 5 miles
Day 2 (hard): 5 to 8 miles
Day 3 (easy): 2 to 5 miles
Day 4 (hard): 5 to 8 miles
Day 5 (easy): 2 to 5 miles
Day 6 (easy): 2 to 5 miles
Day 7 (hard, long-run day): 10 to 12 miles

Week's total mileage: 28 to 48 miles

Fast Running

As you become comfortable with the distances you're covering on days 2 and 4 (hard days), you'll be ready to add variety to your program, including some form of fast running. Or you can opt to increase your mileage on days 2 and 4, still keeping the total for those days lower than the run on day 7.

Many women will stabilize their running programs at this point, running 30 to 40 miles a week, never stepping on a track or running with a stopwatch. Now they can confidently enter an occasional road race, knowing that they will easily cover the distance because they routinely run that far on a hard day.

Other women will find 30 to 40 miles a week a good training base if they decide to sharpen their program with speed work or by adding more mileage to prepare for a longer racing distance or to improve their times over shorter distances.

More sophisticated training systems will be discussed in Chapter 7.

WARNING NOTES

It seems that nothing these days comes without some kind of warning attached. So, too, as a runner you should be alert to potentially dangerous physical symptoms which must be heeded.

If you're getting ahead of yourself in your training, you may develop any

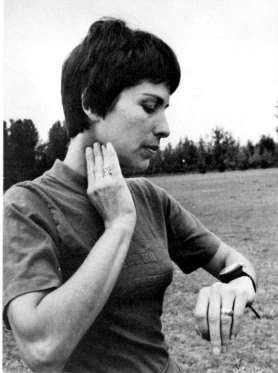

To check your pulse rate, press your fingertips either against the radial artery located in the wrist, just below the base of the thumb (left), or against the neck's carotid artery, underneath the back of your jaw (right).

of the following symptoms while running: dizziness, nausea, loss of muscular control, pronounced breathlessness, or a feeling of tightness or pain in the chest. Regard any of these symptoms as a stop sign. Stop exercising immediately. If the symptoms persist, seek medical attention. In most cases, they will disappear when you stop pushing yourself too hard too soon.

A quick check of your pulse can tell the story. Within 5 minutes after exercise, your pulse should be approximately 120 beats per minute or less. After 10 minutes it should have dropped to 100. If your pulse is too high, you're working too hard. Remember: Train, don't strain.

RUNNING FORM

Running form is important, but it shouldn't get in the way. Remember, it's not how you run that counts, it's the fact that you do run.

Bill Bowerman advises that the "best postural position for a distance runner is an upright one. A line from the ear straight down to the ground should show the back is perpendicular to the ground while running." You should run with a straight back, neither leaning forward nor arching backward. Run tall, as if someone were holding you up by a string attached to your head. Your buttocks should be tucked in, your head up; look at the horizon. And open your mouth when you run; breathing is much easier that way.

Your arms should be relaxed, with the elbows held slightly away from your body—neither flapping like wings nor pressed to your chest—and bent at close to a 90-degree angle. Let your arms swing freely, your wrists passing in an arc between your hipbone and your bust line. Your shoulders should be level and your hands relaxed, loosely cupped; no tightly clenched fists.

Carry your arms at a comfortable height; let them swing freely, and keep your shoulders relaxed.

A beginning runner should concentrate on running flat-footed, or even heel-toe, in an effort to avoid the toe running (actually landing on the ball of the foot) normally associated with sprinting. It's not terribly important whether you land flat-footed or heel first, just that you stay off your toes. The ball of your foot should not be absorbing the first impact of your foot strike. Instead, the impact should start at the back of your foot, move to the ball, and finally to the toes as you push off again.

Try to maintain good posture when you run. Run erect and stay as relaxed as possible. Keep your hips and pelvis under you.

Common Problems

Owing partly to their anatomy and partly to athletic inexperience, women runners often have one or two of the following problems with form:

Swayback, buttocks sticking out. It's not easy to correct swayback, but think about running with your pelvis tucked under you. Try abdominal exercises to strengthen the abdominal muscles, which help pull your buttocks under you.

Knock-kneed, legs kicking out to the side. A woman's wider pelvis often prevents her legs and knees from forming a straight line down from her pelvis, forcing the knees to turn in. Think about running in a straight line, bringing your feet under your body, not out to the side.

Arms hugged to the chest, shoulders hunched. Relax your shoulders and drop your arms a bit. Let them swing through in a complete arc.

Arms too low, never rising above the waist. Bend your arms more and let them swing in a fuller arc.

Running on toes. Think heel-toe.

Leaning forward or hunching over. Run tall, straighten your back, swing your arms through. Keep your head up, shoulders relaxed.

Overstriding. Young girls are often prone to overstriding. Your stride should be smooth and economical, not lunging and off balance.

Your hands should be either loosely cupped or in easy fists. Do not clench them tightly.

Try to land flat-footed or heel first (above). Unless you're sprinting, avoid landing on the toes (below), which puts excessive strain on the lower leg.

Common Problems

Carrying your arms too high causes tight, hunched shoulders, as seen here. Keep your arms and shoulders relaxed.

Try not to run with arms too straight, as shown by the runner on the left. Your arms should form close to a 90-degree angle (right).

Your feet should move in a straight line under you, not out to the side as this runner's do.

Run erect; many women have swayback problems, as shown by this runner with the arched back. Your hips and pelvis should be directly under your trunk, not following you.

Crumbling on hills. Your running form should not deteriorate when you run up a hill. Run tall, and if it's a short hill, bound up with powerful strides. If it's a longer hill, take short, economical steps. On training runs, run up a hill with the same amount of effort you use on flat ground. In races, attack the hills, working hard, then keep up your speed even after reaching the top; float down the other side. When running downhill, avoid high speeds unless it's a very short and important race. Stay erect running down gradual hills; on steeper hills, arch your back a bit and let your shoulders hold you back. If you need to practice running fast downhill, do it on soft surfaces. Run uphill on your toes; run down on your heels.

Running should be natural, but if you haven't run since childhood, you have a whole new body to retrain. Have a friend analyze your running form and pick out gross problems. Think about running tall and running relaxed. The more you run, the more efficient you'll become.

TRAINING EFFECTS

Your two goals as a beginning runner are to establish basic fitness and to make running a habit. As you achieve those goals you'll start to feel the training effect. Let's look at the changes you're helping your body make.

Most of your exercise up to this point has been *aerobic,* which loosely means "with oxygen." Aerobic exercise such as running increases the total volume of blood in your body by as much as one quart. This increased blood supply brings more oxygen to your tissues and carries off more waste products, decreasing fatigue and making you feel more energetic. At the same time, the number of effective blood vessels in your body increases. As those vessels become more pliant, your blood pressure decreases.

As you progress in your training, you'll experience *anaerobic* exercise when you run fast or sprint. Anaerobic exercise takes place when the oxygen demands of the tissues are greater than the amount of oxygen which can be supplied through the process of respiration during that period of exercise. Aerobic activity can go on for a long period of time, while anaerobic activity can last for only a short time.

The more your heart works, the better it works and the stronger it becomes. Your more efficient heart can now pump more blood with fewer strokes. Your resting pulse rate decreases. While the average 30-year-old female has a resting pulse of 70 to 80 beats per minute, her pulse could decrease with exercise to 50 beats or less per minute.

Run tall when you run up a hill.
Drive with your arms and lift your
knees higher than normal. Bound
up short hills with powerful strides.
On longer hills, shorten your stride
but maintain your cadence.

Running tones the body as muscle begins to replace fat. You may not lose weight, but you're bound to lose inches. Because running conditions many of the muscles in your body, including your diaphragm, you'll be able to breathe more easily as the air flows in and out more rapidly and with less effort. You'll be able to perform tiring work more easily because of your increased capacity to absorb and distribute oxygen.

In short, you'll experience a sense of physical well-being. You'll have a new pride in your appearance and the ability to work more and tire less. Most important, your self-esteem will grow dramatically.

3

Shoes and Clothing

Your single most important piece of running gear is a pair of shoes. You can get by in secondhand clothing, but good shoes are well worth their price in terms of comfort, performance, and injury prevention.

RUNNING SHOES

You're never going to know the true feeling of comfort that running shoes can offer unless you try them. If you've been jogging 3 miles a day in aerobic or tennis shoes, you'll feel a world of difference when you start running in a pair of well-designed running shoes. True, you may need an interpreter when you go shopping for the right pair. Air, gel, ZO^2. Torsional rigidity bars, dynamic reaction plates. EVA, PU, kinetic wedges, cantilever outsoles. What does it all mean?

Running shoe technology has produced a myriad of shoes in a continuing search for a lightweight, shock-absorbing shoe with motion control. Early running shoes offered only minimal protection, which was satisfactory for the runner with natural aptitude and a lightweight physique. But with the running boom, the profile of the "typical" runner changed. Running shoe designs reflected the change and tended to help the heavier, slower runner rather than the light-footed elite runner.

Today, each shoe company has its own answer to the runner's needs—whether it be a shock-absorbing gel or encapsulated air in the midsole of the shoe, or a soft wedge in the forefoot to improve the runner's footstrike. Shoe designs change annually—there may be as many as 50 new models to choose from each year. (You may find that your favorite shoe is no longer in produc-

Typical warm-weather running gear includes running shoes, lightweight socks, shorts, and sleeveless top.

tion or has undergone major changes.) Running magazines traditionally offer an annual look at the current crop of shoes on the market, giving in-depth evaluations and information about which type of shoe is best for which type of runner.

Most runners will fit into one of three distinct categories of foot types: low-arched (pronated), high-arched (supinated), or neutral (between the two).

The pronated foot is often a problem because of its excessive flexibility. Overuse injuries such as plantar fascitis, heel spur syndrome, and shin splints (see Chapter 6) are more likely to occur in runners with low-arched feet. Straight-lasted shoes with firm heel counters may help head off injuries.

The supinated foot is more rigid and therefore poor at absorbing shock. Runners who supinate are more susceptible to stress fractures, Achilles tendinitis, and metatarsal pain. Cushioning and flexibility are important for the runner with a high arch; the shoes should be built on a curved or slightly curved last.

The runner with a neutral foot has the ideal situation. She's less prone to injury and may need less of a shoe (in terms of weight and stability) than her high- and low-arched friends.

"Today's shoes are far superior to those available just five to ten years ago," write podiatrists Jonathan Contompasis and Raymond Feehery of Delaware All-Sports Research. "There is an emphasis on good biomechanical design and features designed to minimize injuries. Balancing shock absorption with motion control also is important."

If you're looking for a new pair of running shoes, head for a running specialty store, or at least a store that deals exclusively in sports supplies. You're not likely to find knowledgeable sales help at your local discount or department store. Try on a variety of brands and styles. Let the sales clerk know what your special needs are, and don't be afraid to ask questions.

Are you looking for training shoes or racing shoes or shoes that will be adequate for both?

Stick with respected brands—not cheap knockoffs. Leading manufacturers of running shoes include Adidas, Asics Tiger, Autry, Avia, Brooks, Converse, Diadora, Etonic, New Balance, Nike, Pony, Puma, Reebok, Saucony, and Turntec.

Your training shoe will be heavier and more massive in feel and appearance than a racing flat. You may be surprised, though, at how light a substantial-looking shoe can be. Unless you consider yourself a competitive runner, your training shoes should serve you fine for road racing.

Your running shoe should feel well cushioned and supportive. The upper should be made of a soft material that won't rub your feet raw (nylon and suede are softer than regular leather). Most models typically have a nylon mesh upper reinforced with soft leather or suede. A padded heel and ankle collar reduces friction and protects your Achilles tendon.

Most current shoe models have deeper and wider toe boxes than older models. The more ample toe room decreases the risk of chronic irritation and blistering of the big and second toes and allows runners to more easily use prescription inlays and orthotics. Your shoes should have ample room for your toes to wiggle (with about a half-inch between the end of your toes and the end of the shoe).

Check for a sturdy heel cup. You may also note that the heel is slightly elevated by a ½- to ¾-inch wedge. Some shoes have slightly flared heels for greater stability.

Your shoe will have a midsole that acts as the primary cushioning area and may be the site of all the high-tech inventions that promise you a run on the clouds. The outsole will be made of a harder, more durable material. The sole should be flexible enough, however, so that your forefoot is flexible. You should be able to easily rise up on the balls of your feet. Be aware that many black-soled shoes leave marks on floors; you may have to make a habit of checking your running shoes at the door. The outsole also will have a sole pattern to provide traction, and in some cases, more cushioning.

A typical women's running shoe will weigh 8 to 10 ounces. It should feel firm enough to avoid any sinking feeling at the heel or any wobbly feeling when you're running. By all means, take your shoes for a quick test run on an uncarpeted surface.

Racing Shoes

If you're serious about cutting some seconds off your personal records (PRs), invest in a pair of racing shoes, although you'll find only a limited selection. A racing flat (for road races) may weigh as little as 5½ ounces; a spiked shoe (for track races), close to the same. Both types of racing shoes are built on curved lasts and feel like slippers. They offer less durability, stability, and cushioning than a training shoe, but the less weight you carry in a race, the faster you'll run.

If you are a light, biomechanically efficient runner, you may be able to make use of a streamlined training shoe for both training and racing. Likewise, a heavier runner who needs more stability and cushioning might look to the lightweight training shoe for use as a racer, rather than risking injury with a true racing shoe.

As for spikes, unless you're planning to be a sprinter (racing a quarter-mile or less), you're better off with a spiked shoe that also has some kind of heel. If you plan to race sparingly on the track at longer distances, your road-racing flats should be satisfactory on all-weather tracks.

Men's or Women's Shoes?

Manufacturers offer a number of "women's" running shoes. Some are virtually the same as a standard men's model but with women's sizing and different colors. Others may have been designed specifically with a "true woman's last." It may be easier to find a good fit in a woman's shoe, but if you wear a size 7 or 8 or larger, you may find that you can take advantage of the wider variety of men's models. A man's shoe size is about 1½ sizes larger than a woman's. If you wear a women's size 8, you'll fit into a men's size 6½. A few men's shoes come in sizes 3 to 13; a few shoes—men's and women's—come in widths.

Shoe Care

Your running shoes may be your largest investment in the sport. Be sure to read any manufacturer's instructions for use and care. Here are a few tips:

1. Keep them as clean as possible. Unless instructed otherwise, hand-wash nonleather shoes (machine-wash the laces) and let them air-dry, stuffed with paper towels or newspaper. Change the paper stuffing several times to speed up the drying time.

2. Don't use running shoes for other sports. Running shoes are built for forward motion only and won't stand up under the lateral movement of sports such as tennis, basketball, or handball.

3. Keep the wear on your heels even. Don't let your shoes get so run down that one side of the heel is considerably lower than the other. Worn-down heels can be the first step to injury. Get your shoes reheeled, if possible, or buy a new pair.

4. Wear socks. Although some runners prefer to run sockless, socks are a good idea for hygienic reasons. You can wash your socks every day, and the sweat and dirt they absorb is that much less sweat and dirt for your shoes to collect.

5. If you have unusual feet—with bunions, calluses, or toes that stick out in odd directions—don't be afraid to cut into your shoes to relieve pressure on sensitive areas. A shoe-repair shop can cut a hole at the offending area and put a roomy patch on top, preserving the integrity of the shoe while allowing your feet to strike the ground in comfort.

Training shoes, such as those shown here, are heavier and have more cushioning than racing shoes. Note that all have an elevated heel, a must for distance runners.

Running Shoes

Most running shoes have wide, stable heels and a sole pattern designed to help provide traction (right). There are many to choose from. Shoes with nubs or waffle patterns, such as those shown here (bottom), offer solid cushioning for street running.

Pronation, characterized by inward foot roll (top), and supination, characterized by outward foot roll, can often be corrected by wearing orthotics (below), which are foam or plastic insoles custom-fitted to an individual's feet.

6. Don't try to squeeze extra mileage from worn-out shoes. If the midsole has compressed or otherwise lost some of its capacity for shock absorption, or if the soles are worn beyond repair, get a new pair and avoid injuries.

RUNNING CLOTHES

Once you've obtained good running shoes, you can consider running clothes. Fashion plays a psychological role in running, but it's best to put comfort and function first. With the healthy women's running marketplace, though, you should have no trouble satisfying both needs.

Underwear

From the skin out, your first concern is underwear. Some women can run comfortably without bras and do so, as their own modesty permits. Other women need bras; running without one can be painful for a woman with large breasts. A well-fitted bra can minimize the problem by toning down the violent up, down, and lateral movement of the breasts.

Women's sports bras have been available since the late 1970s and now are offered by dozens of manufacturers, from JogBra to Lily of France to J.C. Penney. Most are made of a nonchafing, absorbent cotton/polyester blend. There are two basic styles: compression bras, which flatten the breasts, limit movement, and redistribute mass evenly across the chest, and encapsulation bras, which support each breast separately in its own cup. Women with A, B, and C-cup sizes can use a stretchier, more comfortable bra, whereas the D-cup runner will need more rigid and binding support.

A good running bra should distribute weight evenly over the rib cage and spread it over the back, rather than using the shoulders as support. Straps should never dig; the cross-back or racer-back designs allow for maximum arm movement. The cups should be seamless or have seams that do not cross the nipple area. Bras that fasten in the front are convenient but often chafe, and they offer less support than those that have back closures or that slip on.

When trying on a bra, do some running in place in front of the mirror; swing your arms in full circles. Breathe deeply. Be critical. If you have chafing problems with your bra when running, apply some Vaseline to the offending spot to reduce friction.

For underpants, choose styles that are nonbinding and that stay in place. Nylon underwear is satisfactory, but in hot weather cotton will be cooler.

(Incidentally, a number of women's running shorts come with built-in briefs so that you don't need to wear underpants.)

Socks

Socks are also a matter of preference. Some people claim socks give them blisters. Others say that they only get blisters when they don't wear socks. But from the viewpoint of hygiene, wear them. They'll also give you some added cushioning and help reduce heat buildup in your shoes in hot weather. In cold and wet weather, they'll keep your feet warmer and drier. In general, wear only one pair. If you wear more, your shoes may be too snug. Likewise, if you suddenly decide to run without socks, your normal running shoes may fit too loosely. Thin socks worn under heavier socks tend to develop folds in uncomfortable places. If you want extra warmth, try wearing a pair of nylon tights, the type worn by dancers. They're very durable and elastic. You can wear them under your running shorts, with or without socks. They'll keep you warm and won't get heavy and baggy in the rain.

A good pair of running socks is absorbent, fits smoothly, and stays in place. The degree of cushioning will be up to you. You may want a heavier, well-cushioned sock for training and a lightweight, thinner quarter-sock for racing or hot weather.

Shorts and Tops

Women no longer have to rummage through the bargain bins of boys' PE shorts to find something to wear for running. The fashion industry has finally joined forces with sports clothing manufacturers to give women an excellent choice of running shorts, something for every figure. Most women prefer a loose-fitting "shell short," often with its own liner. These shorts come in a variety of cuts, and the runner never has to worry about her underwear showing or "her buns hanging out." You'll find the shorts in cotton, nylon, or cotton blends. Sizing is as inconsistent as it is in regular women's wear, and some manufacturers even change their own sizing from one year to another. A medium short one year may be the same size as the next year's small. Keep shopping around until you find the shorts that make you feel your best when running.

Elite runners (or those with an elite runner's figure) often opt for a racing brief for competition. These stretchy shorts are light, snug, and if well fitted, feel like underwear. They also leave little to the imagination. Bodysuits with French-cut legs are also worn by some top women racers, and a growing number of triathletes do their racing in thigh-length Lycra biking shorts.

Attractive, coordinated running shirts/singlets and shorts are widely available. However, two or three pairs of shorts coupled with a drawerful of race T-shirts (short- and long-sleeved) or cast-off turtlenecks or summer tops is usually enough for most women. You may want to invest in a singlet or two for summer running, however. Look for lightweight cotton or cotton blend tops; for extra cooling, try a mesh singlet or a cropped top. Some sports bras come in dark colors and styles that make them practical for wearing alone in hot weather. During cold weather, a few old turtlenecks will extend your running wardrobe.

Outerwear

Shorts, T-shirts, underwear, socks, and shoes will be fine for most days, but be aware that the most common problem for the beginning runner is overdressing: the sweat-suit syndrome. Those beautiful warm-up suits you see advertised everywhere are great for warming up, cooling down, and wearing before and after you run, but for most running you'll have no need for one.

If in doubt about the weather, dress in layers. You can always shed some clothes on the run. You're in trouble if you've got on a one-piece body suit or one thick sweater or sweat shirt. Beginning runners underestimate the amount of body heat they generate when they run.

Hot weather running calls for cautious dressing. If the weather is fine for spectators, it's probably too hot for runners. In fact, heat is the most dangerous climatic problem a runner must contend with, and the important consideration in dressing for it is the evaporation of sweat. Expose as much of your body as possible by wearing loose clothing, preferably cotton. Don't tuck in your shirt; wear a halter top, if possible. If you're running at midday, wear some kind of cap or visor to shade your face. Don't hesitate to run through every available sprinkler and fountain on your running route, or wet your clothing before you start. Take in plenty of liquids before, during, and after your runs. Liquids, along with proper dress and conservative running, are the best preventive measure for heat distress.

Dressing for cool weather is easier because you can always add another layer. The more layers you wear, the more body heat you'll be able to trap. A typical progression of layers (to the extreme) might include tights or polypropylene underwear, running shorts, sweatpants, wind pants, turtleneck, T-shirt, sweatshirt, and windbreaker. And don't forget a stocking cap and mittens, probably your most important apparel because your head and hands allow so

Outerwear

If you're in the market for warm-ups, consider a tailored warm-up suit (left) or a traditional cotton sweatshirt and a pair of Lycra tights (right).

A nylon shell and wind pants over long underwear or a sweat suit are ideal for cold-weather running (under 30 degrees). Note, too, the knitted headband and lightweight gloves.

much heat loss. An old pair of knee socks is great to have along, particularly in races when you're not sure how much clothing you'll need. Wear the socks over your hands and forearms for extra warmth, and when you no longer need them, either discard them or tuck them into your shorts for the rest of the race.

Two new versions of running tights have emerged in the 1980s: the form-hugging Lycra tights popularized by Hind and a more modest European-style running pant adapted in the United States by SportHill. Lycra tights—offered now by most running gear companies—are extremely comfortable, nonbinding, and feel like a second skin. However, their snug fit doesn't appeal to all women. The European-style pant, usually with a stirrup, offers a lean fit in a cotton/polyester fabric. The pants are machine-washable and like the Lycra tights, hold their shape well in wet weather, a vast improvement over the heavy sweatpants of earlier years.

If you live in a cold climate, you probably know about the wind-chill factor that drives freezing temperatures even lower with a strong wind. On cold days, always start a run into the wind, so that you can return with it at your back. If you run with the wind first, you build up a sweat that becomes icy when you turn around and head into the freezing wind.

If you think you will get wet and the weather is cold, you have several choices. Staying warm and dry when it's cold and wet is easier than it used to be. A decade ago wool was the only widely available material that retained warmth when it became wet. Unfortunately, it wasn't waterproof. And waterproof material repelled water on the outside, but only as you worked up a cold sweat inside. With the invention of polypropylene and Gore-Tex, runners are afforded a variety of clothing to combat the elements.

Polypropylene fabrics have a "wicking" function which lets heat from the body move moisture from the inside to the outside of the fabric. There it spreads along the fibers and evaporates rapidly. You can find polypropylene in thermal underwear, in running pants and tights, in running shirts, socks, and gloves. You can also find running shorts lined with polypro, as it's called.

Gore-Tex is a waterproof, breatheable product that adheres, Teflon-like, to other fabrics, such as nylon. Lightweight, comfortable Gore-Tex running suits are expensive but are both rain- and wind-resistant. They'll keep you warm and dry, inside and out.

Unless you're faced with a steady diet of 35-degree temperatures and continuous rain, you can probably get by on rainy day runs in a pair of tights or running pants, a long-sleeved shirt, and a windbreaker. You won't stay dry, but your own body heat will keep you warm. The important thing is to get inside quickly and get showered and into dry clothing. You'll get chilled if you

For wet-weather running, try a waterproof, or at least water-resistant, hooded anorak and a pair of Lycra tights.

linger outside in wet clothing. Your shoes will be wet too; stuff them with paper and let them air-dry. Alternate running shoes so that you always start a run with dry shoes.

A run in the rain can be exhilarating if you're dressed for it. So run in the rain. Splash through the puddles. Look like a drowned rat. Enjoy it.

4

On Being a Woman Runner

You're off and running. You've started a training program, you're comfortably dressed and properly shod, you're beginning to enjoy running. You may also be noticing some obvious and not-so-obvious facts of life.

You've probably discovered, somewhere along the line, that men run faster than women. And that women run differently from men. You may have realized that while the man next door can beat you in a sprint, you can stay with him on a 3-mile run and maybe beat him in a 15-mile road race.

You also may have noticed that your menstrual cycle isn't as regular as it was before you started running. Or that at certain times of the month you feel lean and mean on your runs and at other times fat and sluggish.

Physiologically, men and women are different; no question about that. And in the field of sports, where physiology is the basis of athletic movement, sex differences must be considered. But unfortunately the bulk of sports research and literature deals only with men. In 1971, for example, the American College of Sports Medicine published its 1,700-page *Encyclopedia of Sports Sciences and Medicine;* fewer than 10 pages of this otherwise epic work were devoted to women and sports medicine. While studies on women athletes are steadily increasing, it will still be years before we have a definitive profile of the woman athlete and the long-term effects of her training.

Here is what we do know. First, research clearly shows that men and women adapt to training in the same way. Second, that boys and girls can compete on the same basis up to the ages of 9 to 12.

Sports-medicine researcher Oded Bar-Or adds that at any age around puberty, "differences in body size and strength of early and late maturers *within* a gender group far surpass the *intergender* differences." At the approach of puberty, the performance gap widens as males start to make sharp improve-

71

Mary Decker Slaney displays the form that has helped make her one of the greatest middle-distance runners in the world.

ments in physical performance while females are leveling off. Athletically, a girl is over the hill by the time she reaches 15, or so it has appeared.

Recent evidence suggests that many athletic performance differences have been the result of social and cultural restrictions forced upon the female just about the time she begins menstruating. But with the advent of competitive women's athletics in high school and college, the lure of athletic scholarships for women, the pressure of Title IX and the women's rights movement, sports are becoming acceptable and as much a part of the American female's cultural experience as the American male's.

We have already seen enormous improvements in sports such as running, and the performance gap between men and women has narrowed considerably. Women are reversing the trend that statistically doomed them to mediocre athletic performances after puberty. Interestingly, physiologists have insisted all along that a woman's greatest athletic potential should be reached when she is in her mid-twenties.

Women's athletic records now are being broken at a phenomenal rate, while men's are standing for a longer time. The difference is one of numbers. Many men have been attacking records for years, but large numbers of women are just starting to make their assault. Women's world distance running records took their biggest plunges in the 1970s. For example, the women's marathon record dropped a whopping 32:39 from 1967 to 1977, while the men's time improved by only 1:03. With official acceptance for their sport, more women runners are performing closer to their potential. Still, women had a lot of ground to make up, as the progression of records from 1978 to 1988 shows: The women's marathon record dipped from 2:32:30 to 2:21:06 (almost 11½ minutes); the 10,000-meter record from 31:45.4 to 30:13.74 (more than 1½ minutes). Men's records at those distances fell by just 1:44 and 8.69 seconds, respectively, during that decade. Women are now knocking at the 30:00-10K and 2:20-marathon doors. Those performances have long stood as marks that separated elite male runners from the rest of the pack. It took some 60 years of competition to bring men under 30:00 (1939) and 2:20 (1953).

At the other end of the running scale are sprint marks, where women's records exploded and startled a world that had never expected to see a woman run as fast as Jesse Owens did in Berlin, or, more recently, as fast as sprinter/football hero O.J. Simpson.

In the past, tests measuring female athletic ability may have been improperly weighted, says exercise physiologist Jack Wilmore of the University of California–Davis. He notes that comparisons between "average" men and "average" women are biased because their athletic experiences are not the same.

(A frequently used example: Young girls and young boys can throw a softball the same distance with their nondominant arm, but boys—because they've been taught how to throw—throw farther than girls with their dominant arm.) Comparisons can be made, though, between females who have maintained rigorous lifelong training programs and similarly trained males.

Although it is unlikely that the fastest woman runner will ever beat the fastest male runner, a highly trained woman will often finish in the top 2 or 3 percent of a mixed-sex race. It's not unusual for an elite woman athlete to drop into a small road race or an all-comers track meet and beat all but one or two of the men, or even win the race. In ultra distance races (those longer than a marathon), women are not-infrequent winners in coed competition.

In terms of athletic performance, there are undoubtedly greater differences between the third and ninety-seventh percentiles in each sex than there are between the average female and the average male. Nevertheless, it is important to understand the physical differences between the sexes that relate to running. In most cases, nature has given the male the physical advantage. Yet nature has also given women the capacity—through training—to lessen the effects of some sex differences.

BODY DIFFERENCES

The most visible difference between male and female runners is body fat. Women carry more adipose tissue than men. The average woman's body weight is 25 percent body fat, compared with 15 percent for men. Highly trained male distance runners have readings as low as 3 to 4 percent body fat, and successful female distance runners characteristically register 10 to 15 percent, although some, highly trained, have been measured at 6 percent. Since adipose tissue (body fat) is an inert substance, it does nothing to help you run, while burdening you with extra weight. Running at the correct body weight may bring dramatic improvement in your racing times, but excessive or obsessive attempts to lower weight and body fat past reasonable levels can lead to eating disorders and other health problems.

Exercise and diet can reduce your body fat, thereby increasing your potential as a runner. But since women have more body fat to start with, and need more to maintain appropriate hormonal levels, their optimum body fat percentage will always be higher than that of a top male runner. However, a reasonably fit female runner will probably have a smaller percentage of body fat than her male neighbor who has just started running after 10 years of sedentary living.

Consequently, she can easily outdistance her potentially faster and more powerful neighbor in a long-distance race, since she's carrying less dead weight, and her maximum oxygen uptake will be greater relative to body weight, a definite advantage when performing an aerobic activity such as distance running.

The male skeleton gives men another built-in advantage. With its wide shoulders and narrow hips and pelvis, it is more suited to running than a woman's wide-hipped, narrow-shouldered frame. A woman has more delicately constructed bones, muscles, tendons, and ligaments, and her wider pelvis creates a mechanical disadvantage for running because she must rock more from side to side to balance one step with the next. The sideward movement impedes her forward speed. Her wider hips also cause the quadriceps (the muscles that run from the pelvis down the front of the thigh) to angle in to their attachment at the knee, increasing the chance of knee problems because of added torque placed on the knee as it seeks a straight alignment. It's no coincidence that most elite women runners have narrow hips.

In general, women have less muscle mass than men. Approximately 23 percent of a woman's body is comprised of muscle, compared to 40 percent in a man. This additional muscle and the greater strength potential it provides are due to the male hormone testosterone, which builds up the size of muscle fibers. Women can increase their strength and muscular endurance significantly through running, weight lifting, and other exercises, although the deficiency of testosterone prevents a woman from developing the large, bulky muscles that could increase her speed.

A decade ago the overall incidence of athletic injury for women was double that for men, largely because of poor conditioning, inadequate coaching, and lack of access to appropriate treatment. Now the injury rate in conditioned female athletes is no higher than that of their male counterparts. Injuries are much more sport-specific than gender-specific.

OXYGEN CONSUMPTION AND ANEMIA

Males also have an advantage in terms of oxygen consumption. The average adult male has more red blood cells than a child or adult woman. Up to puberty, males and females have similar numbers of red blood cells, but at that point men experience a raised red-blood-cell production. The average adult male has 15 percent more hemoglobin (the coloring matter of red blood cells and the protein to which oxygen adheres) than the average adult woman and 600,000 more red blood cells per milliliter of blood. The larger number of red blood cells gives a male a higher maximum oxygen consumption rate (max VO_2) and lets him utilize oxygen to produce energy more efficiently than his female counterpart can. Swedish physiologist Per-Olof Aastrand writes that "the most pronounced difference between the sexes is the smaller stroke volume and higher heart rate during exercise of a given severity for women compared with men." World-class male runners absorb 75 to 85 milliliters of oxygen per kilogram of body weight per minute, while the average male absorbs 40 to 55 milliliters. A world-class woman runner can increase her consumption until it is higher than that of the average male, but she will still be around 11 percent below a comparably trained male. Top women runners and cross-country skiers have recorded values in the range of 65 to 75 milliliters. The average woman, on the other hand, absorbs only 30 to 45 milliliters.

The 11 percent difference in max VO_2 is closely reflected in men's and women's world records in distance events. The current marathon records (2:06:50 and 2:21:06) represent an 11.25 percent difference; the 10,000-meter records (27:13.81 and 30:13.74) are 11.0 percent different.

By training, you can increase your ability to carry oxygen. Running increases the stroke volume of the heart, so that it pumps greater volumes of blood (which carries oxygen) through your body and increases the elasticity of your blood vessels, allowing them to accommodate a larger volume of blood. A normal person has a large number of unused capillaries which long, slow running can call into service. The increased number of usable capillaries will allow more blood to flow through the muscles.

It's important to remember, too, that your success as a runner isn't strictly dependent on being the leanest runner with the highest max VO_2 in the field. Jack Daniels, a leading exercise physiologist who has tested elite women runners, adds another component—running economy—to the equation, noting that "any combination of max VO_2 and running economy can lead to similar performances." Running economy allows you to use less oxygen at a particular speed than another runner who has a higher max VO_2. Joan Benoit Samuelson was part of Daniels' test group. She was about average in maximum heart rate, a little below average in her sub-maximal VO_2 (running economy), higher than average in body fat, but extraordinary in her max VO_2 at 78.6. That figure was higher than the 76.9 average that elite male runners had produced under similar testing. Soon after this was recorded, she ran her world record 2:22:43 marathon.

Says Daniels, "The basic physiological systems function the same way in men and women; likewise, training principles should be the same for both genders, and men and women can train and race at the same relative intensity."

Iron Deficiency

The best way a woman can make sure that she has her full complement of hemoglobin is to include plenty of iron in her diet. Iron is a vital component of hemoglobin and of enzymes and muscle cells, as well as the liver and many other cells necessary in carrying on the body's functions. With a moderate deficiency of iron, less hemoglobin is synthesized during the formation of red blood cells in the blood marrow, resulting in iron-deficiency anemia, which seriously impairs the ability to do sustained work. A more modest iron deficiency can decrease concentrations of certain enzymes, causing fatigue and significant but less severe impairment.

Many women are chronically anemic due either to poor diet or to a heavy menstrual loss, which further depletes an already low supply of hemoglobin. In addition, heavy, continuous sweating may increase iron loss by 1 milligram per day. Runners also have losses of iron in their urine and feces. Under normal conditions the adult female stores only 250 milligrams of iron, while an average male stores some 850 milligrams. A woman with heavy menstrual bleeding has relatively small iron reserves to rely upon. In addition, some studies indicate that women (and men) who engage in strenuous activity may need a larger iron intake than others.

Sports medicine authority Gabe Mirkin, M.D., says that as many as one out of every four female athletes is iron deficient. Likewise, Swedish researcher Asa Kilbom found a 25 percent decrease in iron in the blood of women following a six-to eight-week conditioning program. Dorothy Harris, a researcher at Penn State, found that 32 percent of a moderately active group of women in one locale were anemic, whereas only 8 percent of the sedentary women in the study were deficient in iron.

Exercise physiologist/marathoner Russ Pate of the University of South Carolina recommends that all women athletes get a blood test at the beginning of their training program. Routine checks, especially when you feel "stale" for unexplained reasons, can relieve a lot of anxiety. Too many athletes confronted with poor performance, tiredness, and a lack of motivation misread a physical problem for a lack of mental toughness.

You may feel relatively normal and able to follow your regular training schedule and still be anemic. Or you may have it bad—when hills seem to be mountains, your legs become dead weights, and you get only a 75 percent return for a normal effort. Symptoms to watch for include pallor, fatigue, unexplained drops in athletic performance, and a lack of progress in training effect. A trip to the doctor or medical lab can identify iron deficiency. Be aware, however, that the simple and inexpensive test of hemoglobin or hematocrit can only pinpoint true anemia, stage three of iron deficiency. To detect stages one and two, a more expensive blood screening must be done to check serum ferritin levels (iron stores).

At stage one of iron deficiency all blood tests will be normal except the ferritin level. A level below 20 nanograms per deciliter indicates a decrease in the amount of iron stored in the bone marrow. At this stage a runner may find herself tiring more quickly than usual because of excess lactic acid production.

Stage two sets in after the bone marrow is exhausted of its iron stores and there's not enough iron to form all the necessary red blood cells. Again, the runner will tire sooner than normal. Blood tests at this stage show a decrease in serum iron and transferrin saturation and an increase in the total binding capacity.

Stage three, called anemia, finally shows up in hemoglobin when it drops below 12 milligrams per deciliter of blood in a woman. Pate believes that while only a small percentage of athletes are anemic in the classic sense, a substantial number have hemoglobin concentrations that are less than optimal for endurance performance. Women have a normal hemoglobin range of 12 to 16 milligrams per deciliter of blood, with the average around 14 (men are in the 14–18 range, averaging around 16). In two women who have an equal number of red blood cells, the woman with a hemoglobin reading of 12 can carry only 75 percent of the oxygen of the woman with a reading of 16.

Pate maintains that for an endurance athlete, optimal hemoglobin concentrations are at the high end of normal. However, he tempers his view with two seemingly contradictory notes. On the one hand, he says that given the success of blood doping, optimal levels may be somewhat higher than the end of the normal spectrum. But on the other hand, higher hemoglobin concentrations are not always better because they can increase the blood's viscosity.

Every woman should be sure to get sufficient iron, either in her diet or through supplements. Iron supplements are available without a prescription, but it's advisable to check with your doctor to determine just how much extra iron you need to take. You will need at least the Recommended Daily Allowance (RDA) of 18 to 30 milligrams; any higher dosage should be cleared with your doctor.

There are many iron supplements on the market. Multivitamins, however, generally don't contain enough iron. The best sources are tablets of ferrous gluconate, sulfate, or fumarate that contain 100 milligrams of iron and are usually taken two or three times a day. Avoid the "sustained-release" or "delayed" forms of iron. Also, a vitamin C supplement will help your body absorb the iron.

You should be able to feel the effect of iron supplements within several weeks. Another blood check will confirm the effects of the iron therapy, and your doctor may recommend keeping you on a smaller, but regular, dosage.

Iron supplements can produce an astonishing turnaround in your health, but don't second-guess yourself on diagnosing anemia. Make sure you get your RDA of iron, but don't start popping extra iron pills without doctor's orders. Too many iron pills—or too much of any kind of medicine—can create more problems than they solve.

In most cases, even in stages one and two of iron deficiency, an adequate intake of iron-rich foods will be enough to make supplements unnecessary. The best sources of iron are fish and lean red meat. Dry cereals and bread to which iron has been added are also recommended. Don't let too many "all-natural" foods replace iron-fortified carbohydrates, though. Some foods with a high iron content, such as eggs and spinach, are not good sources of iron because the mineral is not available for absorption. Foods rich in vitamin C, however, help the body absorb iron. A glass of orange juice with an iron-enriched breakfast cereal more than doubles iron absorption. Acidic foods such as applesauce, vegetable soup, or tomato sauce should be simmered for three hours in a cast-iron pot to increase iron content. You should also avoid drinking tea when eating iron-enriched foods because the tannic acid may cut iron absorption in half. Wine, on the other hand, may increase absorption threefold.

If you don't eat red meats, then add vegetable proteins such as chili beans, split peas, lentils, and other dried beans and legumes to your meals of poultry and seafood. Meat-and-starch combinations enhance iron absorption. The true vegetarian may have difficulty consuming enough iron and should consider taking an iron supplement.

MENSTRUATION

Menstruation is not the greatest gift that nature gave to women. At best it's a minor inconvenience; at worst, it's a monthly plague. You're likely to find that your running will influence your menstrual cycle and that your menstrual cycle in turn will affect your running.

Let it be said, though, that women in all stages of the menstrual cycle have won Olympic medals. The cycle itself does not have a significant effect on performance, research shows, although some women do perform better during the follicular phase (prior to ovulation) and others perceive that they do. Problems with your menstrual cycle should not preclude running; in some cases running will even help relieve difficulties associated with your period.

Whether or not the bothersome symptoms related to the menstrual cycle (irritability, water retention, mood swings, anxiety, increased appetite, headaches, depression, and heavy and tender breasts) have a significant effect on a woman's athletic performance is not clear. The problem, in many cases, may be psychological, although certainly weight gain (as much as 5 pounds) from water retention is a factor to be considered by the weight-conscious distance runner.

These symptoms, known collectively as the premenstrual syndrome (PMS), are probably related to hormone levels and/or changes at that time of the menstrual cycle, writes Dr. Mona Shangold, one of the pioneers in women's sports medicine. Exercise is believed to help relieve PMS symptoms; there is also anecdotal evidence—unsupported by scientific studies—that exercise can help women who suffer menstrual cramps.

A survey I made of 50 adult women runners revealed that only 16 percent felt that their menstrual cycles had no effect on their running; many women experienced "good" and "bad" days related to their cycles. Forty percent of the women surveyed felt generally sluggish or bloated before their periods began. Nearly a quarter of them experienced menstrual cramps, and 8 percent said that running helped relieve the cramps. Sixteen percent noted that they felt especially good at certain points in their cycles. Some felt best on the first few days of their periods, some right before their periods, and others at mid-cycle.

One sub-3:00 marathoner wrote, "When I do have a period, I become 'speedy.' The first day or two I am usually awake all night, hyperactive mind and shaky."

A veteran marathoner reported that "a day before I'm due (and the first two days can be the worst) I'm feeling sluggish and crampy, but much better than when I was a teenager."

Another felt "bloated and sluggish several days before my period and the first day of it. I prefer to race around mid-cycle . . . best results then; I feel 'lean and mean.' "

The most frequent problem for women runners may not be menstrual periods themselves, but lack of them. Shangold reports that among competitive athletes, as many as 50 percent are amenorrheic (do not have periods). Infrequent periods (oligomenorrhea) and amenorrhea are more prevalent among athletes (10 to 20 percent) than in the general population (5 percent). Runners are more likely to have these menstrual dysfunctions than are swimmers or cyclists.

Shangold notes, however, that the prevalence of menstrual dysfunction does not correlate with average weekly mileage, running pace, or number of years spent training. In fact, amenorrheic runners have had a high incidence of menstrual irregularities prior to their running programs.

Frances Munnings, a writer for the periodical *Physician and Sportsmedicine,* writes that when researchers first discovered that women who train heavily became amenorrheic, there was a flurry of research to find the cause: "Stress, poor nutrition, low body fat, weight loss, delayed menarche (the onset of menstruation) and the training itself were implicated. Ultimately, although the cause was not clearly defined, this type of amenorrhea came to be seen as relatively benign and probably reversible. The problem then was to convince physicians not to ignore an athlete with amenorrhea, because it was important to rule out other causes of the condition."

If your menstrual cycle starts to vary, don't panic, but do see a doctor for an evaluation in order to rule out a problem that is unrelated to exercise, such as pituitary or thyroid malfunction.

More recently, amenorrhea in athletes has become part of a confusing picture which includes osteoporosis, cancer, coronary heart disease, and estrogen treatment. Amenorrhea can be treated with estrogen replacement, usually in the form of an oral contraceptive, but the treatment has its pros and cons.

Estrogen does offer protection against osteoporosis and reduces the risk of coronary heart disease. Yet it also increases the risk of endometrial cancer. To add to the confusion, research indicates that exercise—in unspecified amounts—helps prevent osteoporosis, lowers cancer rates in women, and reduces the risk of coronary heart disease. Although low-dose contraceptive pills are considerably safer and have fewer side effects than higher-dose pills, some women resist the idea of taking estrogen.

Dr. John Robertson of the Seattle Sports Medicine Clinic addresses the runner's dilemma, noting that for amenorrheic runners who are exercising only for fitness or fun, a 10 percent reduction in mileage and a small weight gain (three to four pounds) will usually allow normal periods to start again. If that fails, he recommends trying oral contraceptives or hormonal replacements. For the competitive runner with amenorrhea, Robertson acknowledges that the problem is not so simple. Many of these runners will be unwilling to sacrifice their training and racing weight in order to have regular periods. Robertson believes, however, that those runners with a history of stress fractures would be better off with hormonal protection from them, through either a return to normal periods or hormonal replacements. The loss of training and competing time due to injury, he points out, is a greater problem than concern over hormonal therapy.

FERTILITY

Research has not shown that athletes have more problems with infertility than the normal population, but Shangold theorizes that, given the higher incidence of menstrual dysfunction among athletes, a transient infertility may be associated with intensive training. The situation usually resolves itself when the athlete reduces her intensity of training. It's not unusual for athletes to go without periods for years, then cut back on their training and become pregnant. Certainly the fact that Ingrid Kristiansen, Joan Benoit Samuelson, and Mary Decker Slaney are all mothers shows that years of intense training did not affect their fertility.

PREGNANCY

Pregnancy and running are not mutually exclusive. As researcher Dorothy Harris notes, "One doesn't have to be relegated to the rocking chair for nine months waiting for the Blessed Event."

On the other hand, you don't need to prove how tough you are by running marathons while you're pregnant.

In recent years pregnant runners have been barraged with conflicting messages. They read stories lauding women who've competed in the U.S. Olympic Marathon Trials while pregnant, women who've kept up their 70-mile weeks through the ninth month, and women who seemingly jogged into the delivery room, then pushed their newborns home in a baby jogger the next day, taking in a 10K road race along the way. Then they see the latest recommendations from the American College of Obstetricians and Gynecologists (ACOG), calling for only 15 minutes of strenuous exercise and not letting the heart rate exceed 140 beats per minute.

What's a prospective mother to do?

For starters: be cautious, listen to your body, and consult with your doctor. The following guidelines, based on information from the ACOG and the Melpomene Institute of Women's Health Research, should help:

• Consult your physician before continuing with your running. There are certain medical conditions that preclude running during pregnancy. These may include a history of miscarriages, placenta previa, heart disease, multiple pregnancies, a weak cervix, high blood pressure, obesity, anemia, diabetes, or thyroid disease.

• Don't try to start a more rigorous training program. Be prepared to cut back on intensity and distance. Never push yourself to exhaustion.

• For maximum benefit, exercise at least three times weekly, for 20 to 30 minutes. Keep your heart rate in the 120 to 140 range, or 25 to 30 percent lower than normal. Your resting pulse should be back to normal 10 minutes after you stop running, but remember that your resting pulse will rise during pregnancy. Use the "talk test" to keep your pace conservative: You should always be able to carry on a conversation while running.

• Don't get overheated. Drink plenty of fluids. An increase in body temperature can harm the fetus, which has no mechanism to cool itself. Dehydration can interfere with blood circulation and may trigger premature labor.

• Avoid the temptation to compete in the normal sense. Become a fun-runner. Be willing to stop if you feel as if you're straining, you become excessively fatigued, or you have any of the following symptoms: breathlessness, dizziness, vaginal bleeding, headache, muscle weakness, nausea, chest pain or tightness, back pain, pubic pain. Consult your physician.

• Include slow, gradual stretching as part of your warm-up and cool-down. Kegel exercises for the pelvic muscles are also recommended, both prenatally and postpartum.

• Don't try to lose weight by exercising during pregnancy. Concentrate on a balanced diet. You need to meet the caloric needs of yourself, your baby, and your exercise.

• Strenuous exercise, if done at all, should not exceed 15 minutes in duration.

• Do not run if you have a fever; do not run in hot, humid weather.

• Get psychological support for your decision, whether you decide to run/exercise or not.

• A lightweight maternity girdle offers support for the back and ligaments; maternity support stockings also help some women feel more comfortable running.

• Stop and walk if necessary because of heat, ligament or joint pains, or Braxton-Hicks contractions.

The Melpomene Institute surveyed 195 women who ran during their pregnancies and found that the "most consistent benefit of exercise during pregnancy is psychological. Women feel regular exercise during pregnancy allows them to have control over their bodies at a time of profound bodily changes. It gives them a chance to relax and helps them maintain a positive self-image."

A later Melpomene pregnancy survey included runners, swimmers, and non-exercising women. The data showed that runners, on the average, delivered at 38.8 weeks, compared to 40 weeks for swimmers and non-exercisers. Non-exercising women experienced the shortest labors (average time was 7.86 hours). Runners averaged 10.25 hours, swimmers 13 hours. The difference in labor duration may have been a reflection of differences in parity among the groups. Three quarters of the non-exercisers had delivered other children, compared to one third of the swimmers and half of the runners. The runners listed pain, fatigue, apprehension, and urinary frequency as the primary problems associated with exercise during pregnancy. They cited the primary benefits as psychological, weight control, and quick recovery.

It's clear that you'll have to make changes in your running when you're pregnant. If you follow the guidelines listed, there's little chance of complicating your pregnancy or harming the fetus. My obstetrician, Dr. Randall Lewis, has among his patients a number of runners, ranging from joggers to Mary Decker Slaney. His main concern is that social pressure to exercise and the competitiveness of some women cause them to put their running goals ahead of fetal health.

Lewis says that it's the "mileage-no-matter-what" mentality that worries him. "If common sense prevails, running is OK," he said, "but people need to be tuned in to themselves."

Ironically, the running-related health problems that Lewis sees are most frequently basic running injuries, not fetal problems. Women who persist in pushing their training despite balance problems and weight gain often wind up with pelvic discomfort or knee problems.

To a large extent, your prepregnancy fitness will determine your running during pregnancy. Remember that Samuelson and Slaney can click off easy 6:30 or 7:00 miles during their pregnancies because they're used to clicking off easy 5:45 to 6:00 miles when they're not pregnant. Of the 195 women runners surveyed by Melpomene, the prepregnancy mileage ranged from 3 to 80 miles per week. During the ninth month of pregnancy the range was 0 to 60 miles per week. If you normally run 75 miles a week at a 7:00 pace for a steady run, then 40 miles a week at an 8:00 pace may be no problem when you're six months pregnant. If you're normally a 20-mile-a-weeker at a 9:00 pace, then your pregnancy comfort zone may be 15 to 20 miles a week at 10:00 mile through your second trimester, winding down to 5 to 10 miles a week of jogging or walking.

Because of the disparity in intensity of training in prepregnancy days, Dr. Shangold disputes the 140-beat-a minute guideline for pregnant runners. She too stresses moderation in exercise during pregnancy but says that "moderate" can't be translated into a certain heart rate or percentage of max VO_2. Recommending 30 minutes of moderate exertion as a benchmark, she advocates perceived exertion as a guide: "If your running pace feels too hard, simply back off and run more moderately. Don't fret about heart rates."

Because of a history of irregular periods, some women breeze through the first trimester without knowing that they are pregnant. Or they may have an unexpected drop in performance. Ingrid Kristiansen, running a (slow for her) 2:33 marathon, didn't feel quite right, then found out the reason: she was pregnant. Other women will find first-trimester running to be near impossible because of nausea during the day. Weight gain and the change in her center of gravity will catch up with the pregnant runner in her second and third trimesters. Three fourths of the women in the Melpomene survey reported some kind of discomfort while running, ranging from pelvic and abdominal pain to sore legs and knees, lower-back pain, and contraction cramps. Weekly mileage dropped slightly in the first six months; by the last trimester mileage took a plunge, and almost 60 percent of the respondents stopped running at some point before delivery. Nearly half of the women raced while pregnant, but almost all said they ran with reduced intensity.

I ran little during the first trimester of both my pregnancies because of extreme nausea. I resumed running in the second trimester and did some low-key racing, about 2 minutes per mile slower than normal. I continued with token jogging, despite severe contraction cramps, until approximately two weeks before delivery. In retrospect, I was probably the kind of mileage-no-matter-what person my doctor was referring to. Even racing at a slower pace, I still could not quite quell my normal competitive instincts. Finding out that another woman in my Lamaze class was planning to run the big local 10K race only made me want to go out and beat her! As for running in great discomfort during the final month or two, I suspect I was only trying to somehow show how tough I was.

Although women who continue to run during pregnancy are more likely to have earlier deliveries and lighter-weight babies, there's no evidence to show that those babies are any less healthy than those of nonrunning mothers. Researcher James Clapp of the University of Vermont College of Medicine sums up the current state of knowledge concerning the exercise-pregnancy link: "Nothing very bad *or* good seems to happen when women continue to exercise at their usual levels during pregnancy."

POSTPARTUM RUNNING

Much has been made of women whose athletic achievements have reached new heights following their maternity leaves (popularized, of course, by the same media which regularly identify women as "mother of two" or "grandmother of six" while seldom affording men such recognition). We hear of Kristiansen, who ran a 2:27 marathon just five months postpartum, and then a world record 2:21 just as her son approached the "terrible two's." Or of Evelyn Ashford and Valerie Brisco-Hooks, Olympic sprint champions, who ran their fastest times after maternity leaves.

While few of us have Olympic medals or world records on our minds as we exit the maternity wing, it is gratifying to know that, thanks to running, it won't take long to reclaim our prepregnancy figures. But don't feel pressured to embark upon a crash postpartum training program. Your running should be a refreshing and relaxing change of pace as you begin life with a new—and demanding—member of the family. This is the time to focus your energies on your baby. Your running can wait.

Lewis advises his patients to wait four weeks after delivery before resuming their running, based on the time it takes your cardiovascular system to get back to normal. You also will have vulnerable joints and ligaments for several months after childbirth. The hormone produced during pregnancy causes connective tissue to soften; excessive stretching or pounding can cause injury.

Don't be dismayed if your first postpartum runs feel like the last few miles of a marathon. With a gradual and consistent training program, you'll eventually get back to your normal pace.

Lorraine Davis, an associate professor of health at the University of Oregon, ran throughout both her pregnancies with few problems, but found that postpartum adjustments were trying. She ran faster when she was six months pregnant than she did four months after delivery.

"I was back at work two days after delivery and trying to nurse," Davis said of her first pregnancy. "Trying to get my schedule organized was my main problem. I waited eight weeks before running again, although I did some walking. I found that I had to jog after I nursed. If my timing was off, I'd go out for a jog and my milk would be running down my legs! I'd lose the milk and the baby would be upset when I returned home and didn't have enough to feed him."

Breastfeeding is a personal choice, and for the runner it has advantages and disadvantages. Although some sources suggest that breastfeeding delays getting back to a normal weight, my personal experience, and that of my running friends, is the opposite. We used to joke that we should become wet nurses as the ultimate weight control method. The extra 500 calories a day needed for milk production seemed to speed our return to normal weight. However, having to spend your early-morning, pre-race warm-up time sitting in a car nursing your baby may not appeal to everyone.

Breast pumps are useful for the nursing runner, especially if she has to run at a time when her breasts would normally be engorged. She can relieve the pressure and store the milk for a future occasion when baby is hungry and she's not on hand to nurse.

The Melpomene Institute offers a number of suggestions for postpartum exercising women who've had uncomplicated vaginal deliveries:

• If you had an episiotomy, wait until all soreness is gone before exercising vigorously.

• If you exercise and begin to bleed heavily, and/or with bright red blood, you should give yourself more time to recover before starting an exercise program again.

• Fatigue is a common problem for new mothers. Consider taking a nap instead of exercising.

• Nursing mothers need lots of fluids.

• Nursing mothers need good breast support during exercise. An elastic bandage over a nursing bra may help.

• Often, women are surprised to find themselves incontinent after delivery. The problem can last for several months. Kegel exercises for the pelvic floor, usually taught in Lamaze and other childbirth classes, are recommended to help correct the condition.

• Sometimes the cumulative effects of pregnancy, labor, and carrying a newborn lead to back pain. Watch your posture and do some abdominal strengthening exercises.

• Maintain good nutritional habits. Don't try to hurry weight loss.

Making time for a run may be the most difficult part of being a running mother. You can no longer take off at your pleasure. You need to find someone to watch your baby; you may need to time your run around a nursing schedule.

Pregnancy is no reason to stop running, as Mary Decker Slaney demonstrates. Many women find that after becoming mothers, they can resume their running careers stronger than ever.

You may at times want to take your baby along, in a stroller or a baby jogger (a stroller designed to be pushed by a runner). However, for the benefit of your own mental health, you may want to make your running time sacred. Schedule it; get a firm commitment from your spouse or a baby-sitter so that you *can* make time for your run. Just as you cherish your new child, you'll also cherish a few moments of peace each day, a time to feel unfettered and free.

CONTRACEPTION

Running may seem to be a natural means of birth control if your menstrual cycle is severely disrupted, but it isn't, and don't be fooled: the fact that you haven't had a period recently doesn't preclude the possibility that you could become pregnant.

Diaphragms are the preferred contraceptive of women runners, probably because there are no side effects related to running. Users of barrier methods must be conscientious and, of course, use a contraceptive foam or jelly in combination with the diaphragm, cervical cap, or condom.

Intrauterine devices are convenient but can provoke cramps and heavy bleeding, which could contribute to anemia. They're also usually best tolerated by women who've had children.

Oral contraceptives have fallen from favor among athletes. Recent studies at the University of Salford in England confirmed what many women had suspected: the Pill reduces maximum oxygen consumption by as much as 11 percent. It also may cause hyperventilation or shortness of breath during vigorous exercise. Increased lactic acid production also reduces muscle efficiency. Additional problems, such as weight gain and nausea, contribute to the unpopularity of oral contraceptives, although Shangold points out that those problems were largely associated with higher-dose pills. Lower-dose pills are now widely available and help reduce a number of problems, including heavy bleeding and the risk of some types of cancer, benign breast disease, and rheumatoid arthritis.

Runners who rely on the rhythm method may soon become parents. Research indicates that many women runners have a shortened luteal phase in their menstrual cycles during intense training. The time from ovulation to onset of the flow is reduced from a "normal" 12 days to about 8, thus allowing fewer "safe" days for unprotected intercourse.

Of course, the AIDS (Acquired Immune Deficiency Syndrome) epidemic has made the condom *the* contraceptive of choice, particularly among the nonmonogamous. While no condom is 100 percent safe in preventing pregnancy, if used properly it can help prevent the spread of AIDS between sexual partners. For further information about AIDS, call your nearest AIDS hotline.

Research is in progress to help answer questions about the woman runner. But until the conclusions are in, you will be wise to follow a training program of moderation. Stay healthy, consult your doctor when necessary, and remember: Train, don't strain.

5

Diet and Running

While many Americans delve into the murky waters of diet pills, celebrity diets, and mega-dosage vitamin programs, the only proven way to lose weight is the standard, mundane system of consuming fewer calories than you burn. And no one yet has come up with a replacement for the "basic four" balanced daily diet that we've been taught since first grade.

THE BASICS

Here is a quick summary of the four basic food groups.

Milk. Milk provides high-quality protein, plenty of calcium, and several important vitamins. Children under 9 years of age need two to three cups of milk a day; from 9 to 12 they should have three cups or more; teenagers need four or more; adults, two or more. Milk products (cheese, ice cream) also help provide your daily requirement. Low-fat dairy products will give you the same amount of nutrition, with fewer calories.

Breads, cereals, and starchy vegetables. Whole-grain and enriched-grain products are the best foods in the carbohydrate group. You need four or more servings a day from this category. If you're trying to lose weight, cut back on the extras (sugars and fats) that often go with these products, in the form of butter, jam, sugar, and cream.

Fruits and vegetables. Fruits and vegetables supply vitamins and minerals. Fruits are also good sources of carbohydrates, which are needed for energy. Vegetables such as parsley, tomatoes, and peppers are rich in vitamin C, as are the citrus fruits. You need four or more servings of vegetables and fruits daily, including one citrus fruit, and one dark green or yellow vegetable every other

No matter how much or how little you run, you should
maintain a balanced diet.

day. Raw vegetables may provide more nourishment than cooked ones.

Meat (especially liver), fish, and poultry are the best sources of complete protein and the B vitamins. You need two or more servings of protein a day. Small (4-ounce) servings of extra-lean beef, a source of what nutritionists call "complete" protein, two to three times a week, are recommended by sports nurtitionist Nancy Clark. Vegetarians need to be creative and diligent to ensure that they get their daily allotment of complete protein from non-meat sources such as dairy products, eggs, nuts, legumes, and various combinations of incomplete-protein foods of vegetable origin, such as potatoes and cereals. For example, rice and beans are each incomplete-protein sources, but together they are a complete-protein source.

Americans typically consume 40 to 50 percent of their calories in the form of fat. The recommended level is 30 to 35 percent. Runners need plenty of calories from carbohydrates, anywhere from 55 to 65 percent. Protein needs are important but are easily met by small servings; calories from protein should represent about 15 percent of your daily intake.

SPECIAL CONCERNS

Besides maintaining a balanced diet and meeting any special deficiencies ascertained by your doctor, your main concerns as a woman runner are getting enough iron (see Chapter 4), avoiding dehydration, keeping an appropriate weight, and taking precautions against osteoporosis.

Dehydration worries are alleviated by a conscientious intake of fluids, especially during hot weather. Dehydration causes an excess loss of sodium and potassium, which can lead to chronic fatigue, and during hot weather you should weigh in daily to keep a close check on it. If your weight is two pounds less than normal, or even lower, cut back on your training and up your fluid intake until you've returned to normal weight. When you go on long training runs or daily runs in hot weather, drink up to a pint of water before you train, and stop en route periodically to drink more water or a sports drink such as Exceed or Gatorade.

Weight Control and Eating Disorders

Many women begin running to lose weight or inches. A combination of running and a slight decrease in caloric intake generally does the trick, although the body's metabolism has a few tricks of its own. Theoretically, by creating a calorie deficit (burning more calories than you consume), you're bound to lose weight. For the average woman, a 2,000-calorie daily diet combined with 35 miles a week of running should produce results—something on the order of a one-pound weight loss per week.

You're not going to miraculously shed unwanted pounds overnight. But a well-balanced diet—short on fats and sweets and long on fruits, vegetables, and carbohydrates—combined with a regular running program will produce the desired results. Your muscle tone will improve, your clothes will fit better, and you may lose weight as well as inches. The key is making your dietary and exercise habits permanent.

Severe dieting plus exercise usually spells defeat. Exercise appears to help a sensible dieter lose weight because it keeps the dieter's metabolism from falling from its pre-diet baseline level. The relationship between metabolism and exercise seems to reverse if caloric restriction is too severe (based on a study of obese women on 720-calorie-a-day diets). Some researchers believe that the additional drain of energy caused by exercise causes the body to defend its "set point" by lowering the metabolic rate in order to protect energy stores. Various surveys have come upon women runners whose bodies somehow fuel 10 miles a day of running on less than 1,500 calories a day. Again, it seems that the body's metabolism is trying to conserve energy reserves.

For most women runners, worries about being overweight don't begin until after puberty. The younger female runner should be more concerned with consuming enough calories to balance the 100 calories per mile that she burns up in training. If she's running 5 to 10 miles a day, it's easy to see that she is going to need 500 to 1,000 extra calories to provide the nutrition her body needs for growth. A girl reaches a peak caloric consumption of 2,600 calories a day around the age of 12, when she approaches puberty and menstruation starts. But as she reaches adulthood, her problem will probably reverse. Too many calories means too much growth in the wrong directions, and by the age of 16 a girl should decrease her intake to about 2,300 calories.

Weight can be a continual problem for college runners, who suddenly find that their lanky, slim-hipped high-school bodies are starting to slip into the abyss of middle-age spread, usually due to a combination of normal growth, poor eating habits, and inactivity.

The increasing prevalence of eating disorders and unrealistic perceptions of body weight, especially among young women, are problems that the running world must face. Collegiate coaches estimate that one third of their runners stuggle with food/weight issues. Running doesn't cause eating disorders, but it may trigger them in persons who already have a strong predisposition. Nancy

Clark, who counsels runners with eating disorders, sets forth guidelines for managing or perhaps heading off these problems.

"Many eating disorders (such as anorexia nervosa—starving—and bulimia—bingeing and vomiting) stem from deep-seated psychological problems and require the additional skill of a therapist. However, some eating problems frequently stem from lack of commonsense nutrition guidance," notes Clark.

If you feel you have a weight problem and/or a food obsession, get an evaluation from a professional. Clark recommends that a physician, with help from a registered dietician, obtain a weight and diet history of the patient, measure body fat with skinfold calipers, calculate a reasonable body fat goal (probably in the 10 to 20 percent range for women runners), estimate daily caloric needs, and design a weight-reduction plan making use of the American Dietetic Association food exchange list (see Appendix).

Clark encourages her clients to first establish and stabilize a normal three-meal-a-day eating pattern. She then creates a weight-reduction plan that corresponds to the new intake, allowing for a variety of foods (through exchanges) rather than a set menu.

"Eating disorders disappear with time. Athletes should routinely plan meals for the day, purchase appropriate foods and set aside time to eat on a regular schedule. Only with planning and practice do eating-disordered athletes bring order to their meal schedule," she maintains.

"I educate my clients on the importance of each type of food. Milk and dairy products are a good source of calcium to maintain strong bones, enriched breakfast cereals provide iron to prevent anemia and fatigue, and breads and grains provide carbohydrates for glycogen replacement. They gradually see food as an investment in their athletic abilities and become more willing to enjoy food for its benefits."

Full-blown eating disorders, as Clark says, must be dealt with by a therapist. Dr. Jack Katz describes the classic future anorectic patient as a girl in her teens, "most likely approaching 14 or 18 years of age (that is, about to make a significant transition in her schooling). She has seemingly been a well-functioning girl, indeed is often described by her parents as having been 'perfect . . . never a problem.' She is highly conscientious about her schoolwork, appears to have friends, and is usually well organized. But beneath this veneer of health, there is often found a girl with low self-esteem, one who is compulsive in her style, works excessively conscientiously to maintain her grades (that is, is an 'over-achiever'), and is overly dependent in her relationships. She is also, more often than not, slightly overweight and has a 'sweet tooth.' "

A stressful event (such as parental death or divorce, a failed romance) usually sets off conscious dieting in "typical fashion." "What makes her different," writes Katz, "is the intensity of her drive to lose weight, her stoic pleasure in enduring hunger pains, and her increasing preoccupation with achieving thinness at the expense of all other goals."

Praise from friends for her willpower and improving figure, and in many cases, faster times for the runner, only drive her further and further "into her ever-downward spiral."

Denial is common among those with eating disorders. But an observant parent, friend, or coach can see the symptoms and urge therapy. The clues: self-imposed, rigidly enforced dietary restriction, substantial weight loss, excess concern with losing control over eating and becoming fat, obsessional preoccupation with food, and distorted body image. Amenorrhea, obsessive physical activity, insomnia, cold intolerance, use of diuretics and laxatives, and involvement with food-related activities (cooking for others, but eating nothing herself; being a waitress; having elaborate rituals surrounding her own food preparation and eating) may also be involved.

The competitive runner is certainly under pressure to be lean, but it is not such pressure, per se, that will cause her to develop an eating disorder. The reasons would exist without running. And on a brighter note, Katz writes that perhaps athletics can be protective against the emergence of an eating disorder: "Those with conflicts over control and self-identity may seek solutions in exercise and sports competition or in weight control or possibly both. Statistically, though, this group must certainly represent a very small percentage of the vast numbers, male and female, who engage in athletic activities."

Osteoporosis

The link between exercise and osteoporosis has two different and intriguing aspects. Osteoporosis, meaning "porous bones," is the gradual loss of bone density, resulting in fractures. Until recently the problem was largely associated with postmenopausal women. Now it appears that recurring stress fractures in amenorrheic young runners are related to osteoporosis because both conditions are caused by a lack of estrogen. On the other side of the coin, regular weight-bearing exercise, such as running, which stresses large muscle groups in both the upper and lower body, appears to help prevent osteoporosis.

Estrogen treatment and a calcium-rich diet can help prevent osteoporosis, too. It's vital for all women to include adequate calcium in their diet, along with vitamin D, which helps calcium absorption. The Melpomene Institute recommends at least 1,000 milligrams of calcium per day for premenopausal women, and 1,500 milligrams if you have gone through natural or surgical menopause. Calcium supplements—calcium carbonate, calcium gluconate, and calcium lactate—can boost a deficient diet without adding fat or calories. Calcium carbonate contains the highest percentage of calcium and is usually the cheapest supplement. Tums antacid is a calcium tablet that is cheap and readily available, but before taking *any* calcium supplement, consult your physician or nutritionist.

WHEN TO EAT

Determine your own schedule for eating and running, but before running, wait at least 60 to 90 minutes after a light meal and up to three hours after a heavy meal. Most people can tolerate morning runs on an empty stomach.

You may find that some foods do not agree with your running. For some runners, milk before a workout produces a "cotton-mouth" sensation. If you eat a protein-heavy meal prior to a workout you may experience some discomfort, since protein digests slowly. Many runners also have a milk or wheat intolerance which, owing to the absence of an enzyme in the intestinal tract to break down those foods, causes abdominal cramping in races or hard workouts. If you have unexplained cramps, experiment by not drinking milk for 48 hours before a race; if that doesn't work, try omitting all wheat products.

RACING AND DIET

The pasta dinner has become the traditional pre-race meal. The night before the big race, most runners eat some sort of pasta, which provides a meal high in carbohydrates and low in protein. The carbohydrates are more easily digested than proteins, and you want a relatively empty digestive tract by race time. The morning of a race you should eat a small breakfast—probably toast, cereal, and juice or fruit—to keep your stomach from feeling painfully empty and to keep your blood-sugar level normal. Try to eat three hours before you race, to avoid abdominal discomfort.

Carbohydrate Loading

Carbohydrate loading, a term tossed around in running circles, refers to the somewhat controversial practice of depleting your carbohydrate stores by eat-

The spaghetti dinner is a popular and sensible pre-race meal. Carbohydrates are more easily digested than protein.

ing few carbohydrates for four to seven days before a long race, then stoking up carbohydrates for the three days prior to the race. Supposedly this loads the cells with extra carbohydrates to fuel you through the latter stages of the race when you've depleted your normal stores of readily available carbohydrates. However, unless you are racing longer than 90 minutes, you will have no need to consider loading. During this period you are fueled by the glycogen stored in your muscle cells, thanks to carbohydrates. When the glycogen is gone, your body has to use fat as fuel, which burns less efficiently than glycogen, making it more difficult to continue to run at the same pace.

Carbohydrate loading can be dangerous because it's easily misunderstood, and the feeling of lethargy that can develop from not eating carbohydrates prior to the pasta dinner is frightening. You can quickly lose all confidence if walking

Aid stations are an important part of any distance race. Be sure to drink the liquids offered at each station to help combat dehydration, a constant threat to the distance runner.

up a flight of stairs the week before a marathon becomes a chore. Some people blow the diet by going overboard with the carbohydrate-loading phase. It's easy to eat too much of the wrong thing and suddenly find yourself several pounds overweight and suffering from an upset stomach. The goal is to keep your caloric intake stable, merely changing the proportions of protein and carbohydrates.

Marathoner Russ Pate notes, "A runner's existence is a lifelong search for carbohydrates." Just don't use carbohydrate loading as an excuse to realize your innermost fantasies of gorging yourself on every imaginable sugar-drenched food.

Fluid Intake

Your biggest concern about your racing diet should be fluid intake.

You may notice a significant weight loss after you run, especially on warm, humid days. Your weight may drop from one to four pounds after a normal run, up to six or more pounds after a long, hot race. Most of this is attributable to water loss, and that water should be replaced—during the day and, to a certain extent, during the race.

Dehydration can creep up on you. Its symptoms include nausea, light-headedness, and a high temperature, which can develop into the severe conditions of heat stroke and heat exhaustion, in the most extreme cases leading to death. So on hot days or on long runs, stop for water during your workouts, and drink up to a pint of water 10 minutes before a race. Consume water during the race as well, up to 10 ounces at each aid station, which should be spaced every 2½ miles. Drink beforehand and early in the race because it takes time for the fluid to get into your system.

Athletic drinks, such as Gatorade, Exceed, and ERG (or Gookinaid), are best taken after the run, since they replenish depleted stores of glycogen and certain minerals. The commercial preparations usually have too high a sugar concentration to be of use to you while running. Since sugars impair the rate of gastric emptying, it takes a long time for the glycogen to get to your muscles, and longer for the water in the fluid to get to its job of cooling you. Sports nutritionist Evette Hackman says that if you're running less than 2 hours at one time, water may be all you need. If you want to use a sports drink while on a run, it should be diluted to a 2.5 percent solution (2.5 grams of sugar per 100 grams of water). For example, you'd need to add an ounce of water to each ounce of Gatorade.

Get used to drinking during races and be religious about drinking during long, hot runs. You can save yourself severe distress.

6

Injuries and Illness

Injuries are the bane of a runner's existence.

You know you've become a runner when the thought of *not* being able to run is infinitely worse than the prospect of having to run when you don't really feel like it.

Women are no less prone to injury than men. In some areas they may be more susceptible because of skeletal design and hormonal differences. But with foresight and common sense, many injuries can be prevented. Prevention hinges on a knowledge of anatomy, proper running form, stretching, proper nutrition (see Chapter 5), good shoe selection (see Chapter 3) and maintenance, and an understanding of running injuries. Let's look at each.

ANATOMY

Vague complaints about a pain in your ankle are hard to answer. But if you know that it is your Achilles tendon that is sore, you can analyze the cause of the injury and move to specific remedies.

The majority of running injuries occur in the lower extremities. Some of the most commonly susceptible areas are metatarsals, Achilles tendons, shins, hamstrings, quadriceps, and knees.

RUNNING FORM

Your legs and feet absorb a tremendous amount of shock, weight, and torsion at each step. As your foot strikes the ground, the shock of the impact is

Running in water has become a highly rated exercise, both as part of a normal training program and as a low-stress form of rehabilitation from injury.

transferred up your leg, so (as explained in Chapter 2) you should try to run either lightly flat-footed or heel-toe to minimize the effects of this pounding. Unless you're sprinting, there's no need to get up on your toes—which invites Achilles tendon and shin injuries. Run erect and in a straight line. Bring your legs under you, not out to the side. Keep your buttocks tucked in, your arms relaxed. Be a floater, not a pounder.

STRETCHING

As good as running is for you, it still causes one problem—shortening and tightening of the leg and back muscles and a resulting reduced flexibility. Fortunately, this can be easily corrected through stretching exercises.

The dynamic action of running causes your leg muscles to quickly stretch, then snap back to their normal state. The result is that these muscles shorten, leaving the typical distance runner unable to touch her toes without bending her legs. This lack of flexibility can be dangerous when you're suddenly faced with sudden stress, such as a steep hill, a fast pace, a long run, or a rough running surface. Your tight muscles no longer have the capacity to stretch, and your body won't move the way it should. The result can be muscle strains ("pulls"), inflammation, or even tears in tendons.

Lack of flexibility can also produce upper-body problems, particularly in your back. So it's important to develop a regimen of stretching as part of your workout.

Before running, always do some light stretching of your upper body, Achilles tendons, and hamstrings. Two or three times a week, whenever it's convenient—at bedtime or just after you run—go through a more rigorous exercise routine, to stretch and strengthen those muscles that running doesn't help.

Illustrations on pages 103 and 104 show simple stretching exercises to do before you run: the leg stretch for your hamstrings, the calf muscle stretch, the trunk twist for the upper body, and the seated straddle-leg toe-touch.

Illustrations on pages 104 to 108 demonstrate exercises you should do two or three times a week: the adductor stretch, the back stretch, the quadricep stretch, push-ups, the sitting toe-reach, and abdominals.

Start your exercises cautiously and always stretch slowly, not so vigorously that it hurts. Bouncy, jerky exercises will only add to the problems that running may have caused. Ease yourself through the stretching, trying to stretch a tiny bit more each time.

Stretching Exercises

This leg stretch will stretch your calves and hamstrings. Plant your heel on a stair slightly below waist level and lean forward slightly. Feel the stretch along the length of the leg. Hold the stretch for about 8 seconds, then alternate legs.

The calf muscle stretch stretches your Achilles tendon as well as your calves. Put weight on the front foot, keep your rear heel planted, and stretch the rear leg by leaning forward with your hands against a wall or railing. Then alternate legs.

The trunk twist is a quick and easy exercise to loosen your upper body. Keep your lead arm straight as you turn, your following arm bent.

Stretching Exercises (Cont.)

The straddle-leg toe-touch stretches the hamstrings, adductors, and lower back. Stretch slowly from one leg to the other without making bouncing or lunging movements.

The adductor stretch loosens the adductor muscles that run from the groin down the inside of the thighs. In a sitting position, hold your ankles and press down on your knees with your elbows.

The back stretch improves flexibility by stretching your back muscles and hamstrings. Bend your knees, if you need to, as they stretch over your head, but try to get to the point where you can straighten your legs in this position.

For the quadricep stretch, take one foot in hand and hold the stretch position for 5 to 10 seconds, then alternate legs. You may want to hold on to something for balance.

Stretching Exercises (Cont.)

Push-ups will add to your upper-body strength and improve your posture. Place your hands even with your shoulders, keep your body straight—no sagging stomach—and lower yourself until your nose touches the ground. Then go up again. If push-ups seem difficult at first, start with your knees in contact with the ground, as shown on the right.

The sitting toe-reach stretches your back muscles and hamstrings. Keep your legs straight and slowly reach toward your toes.

Abdominal exercises will firm your stomach area and help correct swayback problems. Lying down with knees bent, arms back of the head, lift your shoulders off the ground until you feel a tightening of the abdominal muscles. Do not rise to a full sit-up position. For a variation, do this exercise with one leg held vertically in the air and the other bent; or with the ankle of one leg crossed over the knee of the other.

Yet another productive variation of the abdominals is the V-sit, shown here.

Moderation is the key to the strength exercises—the abdominals and push-ups. Start out with a small number of repetitions, and try to do two or three sets. Take a minute's rest between sets of exercises. Alternate the calisthenics with the stretching upper-body exercises, and with lower-body exercises, to form a circuit. As you gradually build up your program, you'll be able to do several circuits at each exercise session.

If you choose to supplement your running with what's popularly known as an aerobic class, opt for the low-impact version. If you run regularly, your concern in such a class should be for stretching and strengthening, not aerobic fitness.

CAUSES OF INJURIES

Running injuries usually fall into three categories: structural imbalance, trauma, and overuse.

Structural imbalance refers to biomechanical problems, such as landing too far on the inside or outside of the foot, having one leg longer than the other, or having an imbalance in the strength of opposing muscles, which can result in incapacitating injuries and persistent disability. A podiatrist or orthopedist can solve many of these problems with foot supports (called orthotics—see page 63), which preserve the neutral position of the foot. Muscular imbalances can be helped by weight-training the weaker muscles to become similar in strength to the opposing muscles. Surgery can be used as a last resort.

Traumatic injuries, such as sprained ankles, broken bones, bruises, and external bleeding, are caused by a one-time known incident. These injuries are treated in the same manner for runner and nonrunner alike, but depending on severity, the runner may have to stop training until the injury heals.

Overuse or stress injuries come in different forms, but they usually appear in the person who is "straining" rather than training. The symptoms of the overtrained runner include mild leg soreness, lowered general resistance (sniffles, headaches, fever blisters), unexpected weight loss (more than 3 percent), abnormal thirst, elevated resting pulse (10 percent higher than normal), fatigue, and poor coordination (general clumsiness, tripping, poor auto driving). All indicate that the runner will be prone to injury if she keeps up her hard training. Overtraining can magnify nuisance injuries and bring on major problems such as stress fractures. Although running is not an unnatural activity, your body can take only so much pounding and jolting. If you push to the point of constant strain, it will break down.

Heed the signs of overstress. Take more frequent easy days. Relax a bit; don't punish yourself for running poorly by making yourself train harder. Watch your diet; monitor your resting pulse and your weight. Don't race to exhaustion. In fact, it would be better not to race at all until you feel your enthusiasm returning. Get plenty of rest and let your body rejuvenate.

COMMON INJURIES

Myriad injuries plague runners. Some of the most common have imposing names such as Achilles tendinitis, plantar fascitis, or chondromalacia. Fortunately, though, many respond well to home treatment or rest. Others will call for medical consultation. If possible, find a doctor who runs or who treats runners; there may even be a sports medicine clinic in your area.

Achilles tendinitis is an inflammation of the Achilles tendon and/or the sheath that wraps around it. When inflamed, your Achilles tendon can be painful to touch and is usually thicker than normal. It will hurt to run, even to walk, in severe cases. The tendinitis can be caused by a short Achilles or a short gastrocnemius muscle (the leg muscle attached to the Achilles tendon); an unstable heel; an inverted heel; a weak arch; or excessive use of the toe flexors. Treatment includes stretching the calf muscles, heel lifts to alleviate the excessive stretching caused by running, and arch supports. Also effective is the application of heat before running, and icing afterward. Try to run on flat, soft surfaces and do not continue running if the tendon is painful. You may have to rest a few weeks (or longer) before gradually working back into your training program. Increase your mileage slowly, trying to stop before the tendon again becomes painful.

Shin splints is the common term for any pain near the shinbone on the front of the leg. Pain along the inside of the shin is properly called posterior tibial tendinitis, and treatment with arch supports, or orthotics, is often effective. Pain along the outside of the shin is known as anterior-compartment syndrome. It may be helped by foot-flexion exercises to strengthen the tendons along the shin. Beginning runners often suffer both types of shin splints if they run on hard surfaces in shoes with little cushioning. Soft running surfaces and thick cushioned soles will help prevent the problem.

Plantar fascitis is the inflammation of the plantar fascia, a tendonlike web which attaches to the heel spur and spreads across the foot like a fan, reaching to the toes. The runner feels as if she's stepped on a rock and may refer to her injury as a "stone bruise." This injury is also called heel-spur syndrome and is generally helped by orthotics.

Stress fractures are tiny hairline breaks in a bone, which rarely show up on X-rays until after they have healed. Tenderness or pain at a particular point is often symptomatic of stress fractures, which usually occur below the knee. Metatarsal stress can be caused by a weak forefoot or Morton's foot (a condition in which the second toe is the longest). Full-foot orthotics that support the metatarsals will help. An unstable heel, a weak arch, or an improper foot plant all can cause stress fractures in the fibula or tibia. A full-foot orthotic helps, but rest is usually the only recourse when a stress fracture becomes very painful. Recurring stress fractures in amenorrheic women are related to osteoporosis and may call for hormonal treatment (see Chapter 4).

Patellar malacia (chondromalacia) is sometimes called "runner's knee." It causes sharp, stabbing pains and tenderness along the borders of the kneecap or under it. Chondromalacia may result when the foot flattens out and transmits a torque to the knee, causing the kneecap to ride slightly out of its groove at the end of the femur; or it can occur because of some other abnormal mechanical alignment that causes an irritation under the kneecap. The irritation leads to a softening of the cartilage under the kneecap and, in severe cases, to degeneration of the cartilage and the development of a rough surface which interferes with the normal smooth-gliding action of the kneecap. Treatment includes isometric exercises to strengthen the quadriceps in order to keep the kneecap on track better, heel stabilizers, arches and full-foot orthotics, and in some cases, surgery.

Ilio-tibial band syndrome refers to stiffness and pain along the side of the thigh. It can occur anywhere from the hipbone to the knee and even a bit below, where the IT band ends. Treatment includes rest, ice, and stretching exercises prescribed by a physical therapist.

Groin pain is probably caused by weak adductor muscles in the groin and the pelvic area. The adductor stretch (see illustration on page 104) will help strengthen those muscles.

Abdominal pains on the right side of your body are usually exercise-induced and result from swelling in the lowest part of your intestinal tract. Therapy is aimed at softening the stool so that gas will be able to pass along the colon. A diet rich in fruits and vegetables helps. Cut down on starches, which yield a hard stool. If the pain occurs during a race, bend forward as far as you can; while still running, squeeze the site of the pain with your hands.

This will push the gas along and help ease the pain.

The "stitch," a sharp pain in your lower rib cage, is sometimes accompanied by a satellite pain in the shoulder. In an unconditioned runner, the problem is caused by an equally unconditioned muscle—the diaphragm. Running will help strengthen the diaphragm, and the problem usually disappears. The veteran runner who suffers from the stitch may be breathing backward or trapping air or both. When you breathe in, your belly should expand. Some runners do the opposite—sucking in their bellies when inhaling (breathing backward). Trapping air refers to tiny bronchial tubes which collapse, allowing air to accumulate in the lungs. Dr. George Sheehan, medical running expert, has recommended teaching yourself to use your diaphragm correctly by lying on the floor with a weight of books on your stomach. As you breathe in, the books should rise. Make it a habit to breathe against a slight resistance. An occasional groan, says Sheehan, is helpful to get maximal exhalation: "Some very good runners grunt and groan with each breath even in long races."

Cramps in your legs during long races may be caused by dehydration or low glycogen or both. A high-glycogen, high-starch diet 48 hours prior to long-distance races, combined with super hydration, will help the problem. Drink water before the race and try to take in a pint every 20 minutes during the race.

Black toenails are common among distance runners, with the big and second toe most susceptible. The discoloration is caused by bleeding under the toenails due to trauma such as pinching or smashing of the nails in shoes that are too tight. The nail turns black and usually falls off a few months after the original trauma. Sometimes the nail will just thicken.

In most cases, black or thickened toenails are not painful but are simply nature's way of responding to extra pressure. You can reduce the problem by wearing shoes with sufficient toe room. If the discomfort is too great, see a doctor for proper treatment.

Blisters are caused by abnormal friction. Do everything possible to prevent them: Buy shoes that fit, break in leather shoes slowly, lubricate your feet with Vaseline, keep your shoes, socks, and feet clean.

If you do get blisters, you can lance them with a needle or razor blade dipped in rubbing alcohol, then keep the blistered area clean. Allow the blister to drain, swab the area with alcohol, and apply a Band-Aid or tape and gauze. You may need to lance and drain the blister several times, always cutting in at the bottom of the blister to promote drainage. Always dip the needle or razor blade in fresh unused rubbing alcohol, and never remove dead skin on the outside of the blister, because it protects the tender skin beneath it.

TREATING INJURIES

You can treat some of the injuries just described yourself. If you experience an acute injury resulting in inflammation (tendinitis, sprains, muscle strains), ice the injured part several times during the first 24 to 48 hours, depending upon the severity of the injury. If you are in doubt about the severity, keep on icing and consult a doctor or trainer. When you are able to resume running, heat the injured area before running, and ice it afterward.

Heat is best applied by using a warm hot-water bottle wrapped in a moist towel, or by soaking the injured area in warm water. Treatment should last 10 to 15 minutes.

Icing of large areas should be done with an ice bag of some kind, preferably a thick, reusable one. Smaller areas can be iced with an ice cup. To make one, freeze water in a paper cup. Peel away part of the cup to expose the ice, but leave enough of the cup to protect your hand as you hold it. After a race or a workout, a handful of ice cubes wrapped in a towel should suffice. Icing should continue on and off for 20 to 25 minutes.

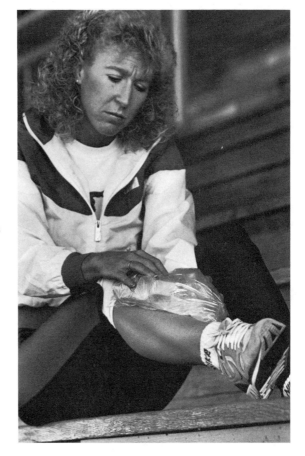

Icing leg muscles with ice packs after working out can help reduce soreness or injury-related pain.

Training While Injured

Some injuries will prevent you from running at all. Some will force you to cut back on your running. Others, such as blisters, may hurt but you can "run through them." Alternative forms of exercise are available for the injured runner who loathes the idea of losing hard-gained fitness or simply misses the invigoration of a good workout.

You can walk, ride a bike, cross-country ski, swim, run in the water, use a rowing or cross-country skiing machine, or ride a stationary bike.

Running in the water (in the deep end of a pool, and usually with a wet vest for buoyancy) has rescued a number of elite runners from lost seasons of competition. Canadian Lynn Williams, hit with a stress fracture in her foot in February 1984, spent eight weeks running in the water from periods of several minutes to several hours a day. She returned to a mix of land and water running and set a 3,000-meter PR seven weeks later. She went on to win a bronze medal in the Los Angeles Olympic 3,000 that summer.

You can mimic your regular land workout by running upright in the water for similar amounts of time at the same perceived effort or pulse rate. You may want to try a fartlek or repetition workout (see Chapter 7), rather than going for "steady runs" in the water. The benefits of water running are so highly rated that a number of runners do part of their normal workouts in the water, both to reduce risk of injury and because working against the water's resistance increases muscular strength.

If you're not overly concerned about maintaining optimum fitness, try to schedule alternative workouts on a regular basis, at least three times a week. By way of comparison, Dr. Kenneth Cooper lists the following approximate aerobic equivalents of running an 8:00 mile:

- Swimming 600 yards in 15:00
- Bicycling 3 miles in 20:00
- Walking 5 miles in 40:00

RUNNING WITH SPECIAL MEDICAL PROBLEMS

Some medical problems described in Chapter 2 preclude running. But many people who have serious medical problems are finding that with special precautions and arrangements, they can still run.

Blind people run marathons. People with multiple sclerosis, people with Down's syndrome, people who've had coronary surgery—they've all run marathons. A teenage girl with epilepsy ran the length of California and Oregon. A man with no feet has run the challenging Pike's Peak Marathon. The New York–based Achilles Track Club was established specifically for athletes with disabilities and has gained national recognition for the extraordinary performances of its members all over the world.

Diabetics learn how to replenish their glycogen stores by following a strict hard/easy program and a diet that includes high-protein meals before running, sugar and orange juice during the run, and a high-carbohydrate diet on easy days. Hypoglycemic runners have high-protein, high-fat meals two or three hours before running, then drink orange juice a few minutes before they start, followed by some kind of sugar drink every 30 minutes during the exercise. Allergy victims learn to pace their running during hay fever season; they avoid races and fast running but continue their LSD running as they wish.

For a person with a medical disability, running is a very real challenge. But with supportive medical advice, the individual can meet that challenge and benefit from it.

COPING WITH THE ENVIRONMENT

Environmental conditions play an important role in running, from breath-robbing altitudes to temperature extremes and the strangling effects of air pollution. There's not much you can do about air pollution except to avoid it, but other facets of the environment can be dealt with.

Altitude

Altitude has a definite effect on running performance, especially for long-distance runners, because of the reduced oxygen in altitudes 4,000 feet or higher. It will take you four to six weeks to acclimatize to moderate altitudes, and upon arrival from sea level, it is advisable to cut back on your training. Then gradually increase to your normal level, running on effort rather than time. If you are going to race at high altitude but can't afford to spend weeks becoming acclimatized, go out slower than usual and count on picking off other

It takes four to six weeks to acclimatize to running at moderate altitudes. Start by cutting back on your training, then gradually increase to your normal level.

runners in the last half of the race. Don't be alarmed by hearing slow times at intermediate distances along the route. Everyone's time will be slower than if the race were run at sea level. Interestingly, many distance runners train at oxygen-weak higher altitudes because they feel that it improves their sea-level performance by increasing red blood cell production.

Heat

Running in the heat requires extreme caution. Dressing properly, as described in Chapter 3, is critical, as is recognizing the signs of heat distress.

Three heat-caused problems to become familiar with are heat cramps, heat exhaustion, and heatstroke. Knowing how to treat these problems may save a life.

Heat cramps are signaled by leg and abdominal cramps, faintness, and profuse perspiration. Emergency care should be taken. Put the runner in a cool place and give her a salted drink or some kind of sports drink. Apply manual pressure to the cramped muscle and stretch it.

Heat exhaustion is characterized by a weak pulse, rapid and shallow breathing, generalized weakness, pale clammy skin, profuse perspiration, dizziness, and even unconsciousness. Put the runner in a cool place and give her water containing salt or a diluted sports drink. Fan her continuously but don't allow her to get chilled.

Heatstroke is a profound and dangerous disturbance of the mechanism, associated with high fever and collapse. It can result in convulsions, unconsciousness, and possibly death. The symptoms of heatstroke are dry, hot, and flushed skin, dilated pupils, and an early loss of consciousness. The heatstroke victim has a full and fast pulse and breathes deeply at first, then takes shallow breaths, and then almost no breaths at all. Convulsions may occur. The body temperature can go to 105 or 106 degrees or higher.

Remove the heatstroke victim to a cooler environment and take off as much clothing as possible. Reduce the body temperature immediately with wet cloths or cold packs under the arms, around the neck and ankles, and wherever blood vessels lie close to the skin. Get the victim to a medical facility quickly.

The most important precaution in hot and humid weather is to be fit and well hydrated. Yet even the fit athlete will not be entirely immune to heat. Drop-out rates in men's and women's distance races were high in the 1988 U.S. Olympic Trials in midsummer, high-heat, high-humidity Indianapolis. At least one runner had to be hospitalized after collapsing with heat problems. The women's 3,000-meter final was run at three in the afternoon—because of television coverage—despite wicked heat and humidity. Mary Decker Slaney and the other runners were hardly reassured by the presence of IV tubes hanging at trackside. Indeed, the third- and fourth-place finishers in the race were on IVs immediately after their gutsy, staggering dive for the line and a coveted berth on the Olympic team.

If you are running and feel the beginning signs of heat distress, slow down, drink water or a sports drink, and cool off. No workout or race is so important that you should risk the effect of heatstroke. Likewise, if you see another runner in distress, you have a responsibility to see that he or she gets aid.

Race sponsors should be prepared to cope with hot weather, but at times there is an appalling lack of planning in dealing with such potential problems. Sometimes no provisions for water or medical attention are made. If you encounter such conditions when registering for a race, give serious thought to skipping it. If you decide to run anyway, supply your own water and have a friend keep an eye on you during and after the race.

Cold Weather

Running in the cold has its own dimensions. Adequate dress is probably the most important consideration; judging the wind is the second. Wind makes cold weather colder; therefore, always run into the wind on the way out and with the wind on the way back. Your biggest problem is not the cold itself but the conditions that come with it—snow-clogged roads, icy pavements, short daylight hours. Use common sense. Dress protectively, get out and run, but immediately after, get inside and into dry clothes.

Freezing lungs is a myth, but frostbite is a danger in extreme cold. A ski mask added to your normal cold-weather running gear offers good protection for your face. Frostbitten skin is cold, white, and firm to hard to the touch. First-aid measures are to rewarm the area quickly with warm, body-temperature water, not with excessive heat. You shouldn't walk on frostbitten feet, nor should you massage any frostbitten area or rub it with snow. Seek medical attention immediately.

RUNNING WHEN SICK

If you feel too ill to run, don't.

It's easy to get caught up in the "never-miss-a-day" syndrome, but if you're too sick to go about your daily routine, there's no point in pushing yourself through a workout which may do more harm than good. Never run if you have a fever.

You can run with colds, and you may even find your congestion somewhat relieved after a run. But don't push the pace when you're under par. Run just enough to feel freshened—not exhausted. When you've recovered from an illness, gradually work back into your normal training routine. Don't expect to be able to take up where you left off.

7

Training and Racing

Running provides a metamorphosis for many women, from jogger to runner to racer. The more they run, the more they want to delve into the sport, to explore their own potential.

Jogging 3 miles a day three times a week will not prepare you for any serious kind of racing. For that, you'll need to set goals, make specific adjustments in your training schedule, and map out plans for racing.

On 15 to 20 miles a week of easy jogging, you can safely compete in fun runs of up to 4 or 5 miles. Just don't get carried away with the crowd and push yourself. And for your first competitive effort, force yourself to run at what feels like submaximal effort.

If you want to compete in longer races but are primarily concerned with just covering the distance, you'll still need to up your mileage. A safe guideline for races up to 10 miles is to cover approximately four times your racing distance in a normal week of running. (If you want to complete an 8-mile race comfortably, you should be running approximately 32 miles a week.) For races of 10 to 20 miles, you should get up to a minimum of 40 miles a week, trying to run at least 75 percent of your racing distance in a single training session every week or two. (If you want to complete a 20-mile race, be prepared to go for 15-mile training runs.) Women preparing for marathons typically run 45 to 65 miles a week, with some runners—fast and slow—able to tolerate 100-mile weeks.

Be aware, though, that more isn't necessarily better. As Bill Bowerman once said, they don't give medals to the person who can run the most miles, they give them to the person who runs the fastest.

When you reach the stage where you want to do more than cover the distance—for instance, when you want to cover it faster—you'll need to add

Whether you're an elite or a recreational runner, racing can be a source of exhilaration and fun.

some speed to your workouts. The key is specificity of training. If you're a sprinter, you train by running short and fast. If you're a long-distance runner, you need a healthy mixture of fast and slow running, with the emphasis on distance. Of course no training program is as simplistic as either of these, but keep in mind your goals and the character of the race you're training for.

Some women make amazingly fast progress, starting out as mile-a-day joggers and then running a marathon a year later. You will have to be your own judge of how fast to proceed. When in doubt, do less. You have plenty of time—the rest of your life—to accomplish your running goals.

You may also find yourself on a plateau at some point in your training. You feel as if you're training as hard as you can but you're not progressing. You may also be fighting a lot of nuisance injuries. It's time to take stock of your program. Consider the following principles from *The Complete Runner,* based on Forbes Carlile's research and conclusions.

Stress: In manageable amounts, stress promotes a positive training reaction. But too much stress will overload the adaptive system, and then the body will begin to break down.

Overload: In order that your body can adapt fully to a particular physical activity, it is necessary to apply frequent and heavy training loads. However, sustained extreme activity, whether in training or in races, should be kept to a minimum.

Specificity: Since your body adapts to the particular type of exercise it receives, your training should be patterned to the particular events you're preparing for in terms of distance and speed. A sprinter should be concentrating on short-interval work, while the distance runner will concentrate on logging the miles.

Regularity: Three or four days a week is the very minimum you should train in order to develop and maintain a reasonable level of fitness. Peak conditioning comes from even more frequent workouts. And remember that not running for even a few weeks can result in substantial loss of your fitness base.

Progression: The most rapid and apparent progression will come in the early months of your running, but your progress will slow as you approach your maximum potential. Further improvement is harder to come by—it often comes erratically. You may be on a plateau and then suddenly come upon the right day, the ideal weather conditions, and the right competition and everything will click.

Diminishing Returns: The first mile yields the greatest return while ensuing miles yield progressively less. Runner-writer Hal Higdon notes that "it doesn't take much to get 90% fitness—only a few miles a day." Substantially more training is required as you approach your ultimate potential.

Women's races are offered around the world, giving you a chance to test yourself against an all-female field. If you are used to running in the middle of the mob in most mixed road races, you may enjoy a heady feeling of success as you run near the leaders in a women's race.

Recovery: "Recuperation periods," writes Forbes Carlile, "are essential both during the single training session and throughout the year." If you intend to train hard for a certain race, you will increase your training for several months, but then return to a normal level or less to allow for proper recovery. Always remember the hard/easy principle discussed earlier.

Seasons: You can't peak continually. Your training and racing has to follow a cyclical pattern of rest, background work, intense training, sharpening training, racing at a peak, and, again, rest. Having off-seasons allows the recovery you need.

Pacing: The basic principle of pacing is that the harder and faster you run, the shorter the distance you'll be able to cover. Conversely, the slower you run, the longer you'll be able to run. Pacing is important both in your everyday workouts and in your overall training schedule, whether it be in terms of weeks or months.

Individualizing: Your training program must fit your needs, your body, your talent, your environment, your schedule, your goals, and your likes and dislikes. Be flexible and adaptable. Experiment and analyze.

With these training principles in mind, examine the racing distance that most interests you. You can run shorter races to train for long races and vice versa, but it's not advisable to try to train seriously for distances as varied, say, as the mile and the marathon.

More and more women too quickly up their mileage to the 70-to-100-miles-a-week stage in their early years of running, trying at the same time to do some fairly serious interval training on the track. The results are predictable: injuries, uncompleted races, little progress, frustration.

A seasoned runner can handle a mixture of high-mileage and interval training, but she must move into it gradually, constantly adjusting the proportion of distance and speed to fit her training and racing needs.

Here is an idea of the type of program you need when you train for specific distances:

Sprints are races of 100 to 400 meters. The 100 and 200 depend almost entirely on anaerobic needs, and training should emphasize sprint intervals of 30 seconds or less or high-speed fartlek training. Sprint training involves an explosive type of running, where speed and strength are essential. Successful sprinting depends a lot upon the natural talent of the athlete, while athletes of lesser physical ability can succeed at longer distances without the natural speed and strength of a sprinter.

The 400 is termed a long sprint, and training emphasizes pace intervals in which the sprinter runs close to race pace but at a shorter distance. The 400 runner also needs to develop an aerobic capacity through fartlek and moderate distance running (3 to 5 miles).

Middle distances loosely include races from the 800 up to 10,000 meters. (Speaking strictly of track races, the 800 and 1,500 would be called middle distances; the 3,000, 5,000 and 10,000 would be called long distances.) All these middle distances call for both aerobic and anaerobic training. The longer the distance, the more aerobic training is needed. The runner builds up middle-distance endurance by running pace intervals, fartlek, and long distance. And again, the longer the racing distance, the longer and slower the distance work.

Long distance refers to races longer than 10 kilometers (6.2 miles). Also called distance races, they range on up to the marathon and ultra-marathon, as long as 100 miles. Aerobic needs are paramount and can be gained through long-distance runs, endurance intervals, or fartlek. Steady long runs will suffice to prepare you for long races, but some form of fast running, whether it is in shorter races or in some kind of moderate interval training, is recommended if you hope to keep lowering your times.

TRAINING METHODS

Once you've reached the point where you can run for an hour easily, you're ready to delve into other kinds of training. Before you start any fast running, however, spend a few weeks adding four to six easy strides at the end of your hard runs. Cover 50 to 150 meters at a brisk, but nowhere near all-out, pace. Jog or walk an equal distance between each hard effort.

A sophisticated training program makes use of several different systems, including intervals, repetitions, tempo runs, long runs, and recovery runs, as defined by exercise physiologist Jack Daniels.

Interval training builds aerobic power by improving your maximum oxygen consumption. It consists of a number of runs performed at a specified speed or degree of effort, with a set amount of timed recovery in between. Daniels suggests limiting your total mileage of fast running to 8 percent of your total weekly mileage or 6 miles, whichever is less. At 75 miles a week, that's 6 miles; at 40 miles a week, it's 3.2 miles.

Each drill lasts from 30 seconds to 5 minutes, run at your current 5,000-meter race pace or slower. You keep the same level of intensity, whether you're running 4 × 1 mile (that is, 4 intervals of 1 mile each) or 16 × 400 meters (16 intervals of 400 meters each). Recovery between hard runs should take less time than the run itself.

Repetition or economy training is similar to interval training, but the hard runs are faster, shorter, and add up to fewer total miles. It also calls for considerably longer recovery periods. Repetitions last from 30 to 90 seconds, never longer than 2 minutes. Daniels recommends running about 5 seconds per 400 faster than your pace for intervals. (If you run interval 400s in 90 seconds, run repetitions in 85.) If you're preparing for races shorter than 5,000 meters, run the repetitions 3 to 5 seconds faster than your current race pace. (If, for example, you can run an all-out mile in 5:20—80-second pace for 400 meters—run repetitions at 75 to 77 seconds.)

Limit the total fast running in a repetition session to a maximum of 5 percent of your weekly mileage and no more than 5 miles total in a single workout. The recovery between repetitions should be almost complete. The recovery will be three to six times as long as the hard run that precedes it (that is, 75-second 400s separated by 4 minutes of jogging/walking).

Hill running and bounding drills also fit in with the concept of economy training, the trick of teaching your body to use less oxygen when it runs at a certain pace. A small amount of downhill running on a moderate incline and soft surface will help you learn how to run faster without having to greatly increase your effort. Keep your downhill runs to a minute or less, and never run at top speed. Uphill running will help strengthen your buttocks muscles and improve your knee lift. Pick a long hill (at least 200 meters) with a moderate grade and run—don't try to sprint—up it. Jog downhill slowly to recover, and repeat. Bounding can help make you more efficient, too. Run a short distance (40 to 80 meters) with exaggerated strides and high knee action. Drive with your arms and spring off the ground after each footstrike. Fatigue will set in quickly; take a near-complete recovery between efforts, ranging from 4 to 8 sets in all.

Tempo runs are hard, steady runs about 20 seconds per mile slower than your current 10,000-meter race pace. Tempo runs typically last about 20 minutes.

Long runs are done at a comfortable pace, about 70 to 75 percent of your 5,000-meter race pace, and should amount to no more than 30 percent of your weekly mileage.

Recovery runs are easy LSD runs.

Daniels breaks his training system into six-week segments, selecting one type of training for primary emphasis along with secondary and maintenance components. Easy runs and days off supplement the program. He advises alternating weeks with three training sessions (the rest being easy runs or days off) with weeks when you run only two training sessions. Races count as training sessions, replacing a tempo run or interval workout.

For instance, in your final six weeks before a 10,000-meter race, you might want to put primary emphasis on tempo runs, secondary on interval training, and use long runs for maintenance. Those six weeks would include seven primary runs—in this case tempo runs—five secondary runs (intervals), and three maintenance (long) runs. You'd have four or five days a week of easy runs.

Daniels' formula provides the basics of a comprehensive training system. My husband, Tom Heinonen, women's track coach at the University of Oregon, loosely patterns his distance runners' training on Daniels' system, although his elite runners typically have fewer easy days—usually three or four a week. Mileage varies for his collegiate runners. The less experienced may run only 35 to 40 miles a week, while the veterans may cover 50 to 60 miles, picking up supplemental mileage from light morning runs in addition to an afternoon workout.

Here is a sampling of workouts, culled from Tom's 15 years of coaching, to add variety to your training:

Tempo runs can be run at a steady pace, as suggested, or at a cut-down pace, in which you run each mile faster than the previous one. This kind of workout is best done off the track, on an accurately measured course (road, bike trail, running trail). You might check with a local road-race director to find the location of mile marks on a certified road-race course. Many exercise trails have mile or kilometer posts. Don't bother trying to measure a course with your car's odometer; it's not accurate enough. You're better off using the mileposts on a lightly traveled road. You also can break up a tempo run with a 1-minute rest between miles. The point is not so much physical recovery as forcing you to complete each mile mentally, with toughness.

Fartlek running can be used as interval or repetition training, or as a free-form combination of the two. Fartlek means "speed play," or running with a constant change of pace. It was developed by Gosta Holmer, a chief Olympic coach for Sweden. Joan Benoit Samuelson enjoys fartlek as a relief from more regimented workouts. She typically uses telephone poles as a benchmark, running hard past 5 to 20 poles, then jogging half the distance for recovery (or sometimes the same distance, depending on the intensity of the hard run). Sometimes she'll run a "pyramid" (5 poles, 10 poles, 20 poles, 10 poles, 5 poles). Oregon collegiate runners often use fartlek to break up a session that starts and concludes with a few long intervals. They might run a hard kilometer, jog, then run 10 minutes of fartlek, jog, then do another hard kilometer.

Fartlek running is perfect for the individual who can't stand the sight of a track or hates to run for time and distance, but who wants to do some kind of speed work. Parks, trails, and other natural areas are the best sites for fartlek running. Look for varied terrain, with hills and flat stretches and preferably soft surfaces. Your run includes different speeds and tempos, from slow jogging or

Training Methods

Long slow distance (LSD) runs are done at a comfortable social pace and help develop a solid base of endurance.

Timed runs, called tempo runs, are done on measured courses with each runner trying to meet a predetermined pace at intermediate distances.

Fartlek running is an enjoyable free-form method of training, involving running at varying speeds over varied terrain. In this sequence the runners are striding hard on a flat section by a lake (above), running easily over uneven terrain in the woods (left), running hard up a hill (right), and maintaining a strong pace over the crest of the hill (below, right).

Joetta Clark (left, #94), Olympian at 800 meters—the "shortest" distance race.

walking to sustained hard efforts for several minutes to almost all-out sprints over distances as short as 50 meters. Running a fartlek with a partner can be a game, with the runners taking turns choosing the speed distance and the rest interval. A typical fartlek run should be 15 to 30 minutes long.

Minute runs are another appealing way to train with less pressure from the clock. The standard form of the workout is to run 1 minute at a moderate pace (5,000-meter race pace), then jog 30 seconds, repeating anywhere from 8

Timed running on the track, whether on interval workouts or time trials, will help you improve your speed and sense of pace.

to 30 times, depending on your fitness. This is a true interval workout, yet it can be adapted to become a repetition workout, with 1 minute of very hard (mile pace) running followed by 3 minutes of jogging, repeated 4 to 16 times. Other variations range from running 3 × 5:00 with 1:00 jog in between, to running 3 × 1:00 (with 30 seconds rest), 2 × 2:00 (with 1:00 rest), 1 × 4:00 (with 2:00 rest), 2 × 2:00 (with 1:00 rest), and 3 × 1:00 (with 30 seconds rest). Minute runs are perfect for working out in unfamiliar places. You don't need a track or measured course, just a reliable watch. You'll be surprised at how quickly the workout passes, because you're so busy keeping track of each segment.

Ins and outs can provide a workout somewhere between intervals and a tempo run. The goal is to run alternate hard and moderate miles (or 800s, kilometers, or 1,200s). You might attempt to run 3 × 1 mile at your 10,000-meter race pace with "recovery" mile runs at a pace only 45 seconds slower per mile. This is a challenging workout.

Chinese Menu workouts are popular with Tom's teams. He gives runners a choice of one to three items from each of several workout plans. The point is variety, giving the athletes a chance to choose something that suits them that day. Each plan is at a different site, all near the usual meeting place for training. Plan A might be on the track, Plan B consisting of a variety of runs on a nearby athletic field, C in a park, D in a hilly residential area, and so forth. Plan A might offer a choice of 4 × 100 meters of striding with 100-meter recoveries, or 3 × 600 with 200 jogs, or one 800 at 3,000-meter race pace. Plan B could include striding the long sides of the field and jogging the diagonals, or 10 minutes of fartlek, or 15 minutes of easy running . . . Imagination is the only limit.

The addition of fast running to your training puts new demands on your body. Ease into training with several weeks of easy striding. Try the more sophisticated workouts once a week for a month or two before embarking on Daniels' program of two or three hard workouts a week. Remember, even elite runners have to follow the hard/easy dictum. They may be able to tolerate three or four hard workouts a week, but they do their share of recovery runs, too.

The distance for which you train will dictate your emphasis in workouts. The longer the distance, the more emphasis on tempo and long runs, and long intervals and repetitions with short rests. The shorter the distance, the more emphasis on short repetitions and intervals with longer rests.

Be aware of the reason behind each workout, whether your emphasis is quantity or quality. I've seen too many runners approach each workout with the idea of running everything all out. You learn quickly that being able to run one 400 all out in 75 seconds doesn't mean you can do it six times with only a few minutes' rest between. Don't be the runner who constantly pushes the pace but rarely finishes the workout.

A typical hard-day workout should include 1 to 3 miles of jogging to warm up, light stretching, a few strides, the workout itself (intervals, repetitions, tempo run, fartlek, etc.), and a 1- to 2-mile warm-down jog. Having a regular training partner or group can make the effort a social event, and you'll find that

the group support will help you along to times you never thought you could
achieve.

YEAR-ROUND TRAINING

The woman interested in road runs has her choice of races throughout the year. Training may vary from year to year, depending on the specific types of races that crop up.

The high school, college, or club runner who follows both cross-country and track seasons will require a more rigid year-round program with different training aimed at each kind of running. The program typically includes cross-country practice September through November, concentrating on tempo runs, fartlek, long intervals, and cross-country competition. December is a month of active rest, of running as much as you like, mostly LSD. January through March focuses on long runs, fartlek, road racing, some interval training, and specific conditioning drills and exercises. April through July training is more race-oriented, with less distance work. You concentrate instead on shorter intervals and then move into faster race-pace repetitions. August is a month of active rest at the end of the competitive season.

When attempting to design your own training program, consider:

1. Your present level of fitness.
2. Your short-term and long-range goals.
3. Your training environment.
4. Your training time.
5. Your training interests.

Your running goals are likely to be ever-changing. For many women, maintaining a year-round base of fitness through LSD and long runs allows them to focus on one or two seasons of racing a year. With a training base of 30 to 45 miles a week, they can move toward the racing distance of choice with appropriate six-week workout programs, as recommended by Jack Daniels.

RACING

Racing, like training, must be approached cautiously and gradually.

The marathon has become the glamour event of distance running, and too many people set their sights on running one before they have ever raced any other distance.

Masters-age races, including this open-field relay, mean you can compete even into your golden years.

If you do have hopes of running a marathon, give yourself at least a year of training for the event, *after* you've reached the point where you can run comfortably for an hour. Enter races at intermediate distances to get a feel for competition, and keep your mileage consistently high (a minimum of 45 miles per week) in the three to four months preceding a marathon. Follow the hard/easy system, and reserve one day a week for a long run, working up to two or more runs of 2½ to 3 hours before attempting the 26-miler.

Road races of all distances are widespread, including many for women only. In the Appendix you'll find several references for race information. Your local newspaper probably runs a road-race calendar in the sports section. You can also inquire about local races at parks, recreation departments, and sporting-goods stores. Pick up a race entry form for details; most races require entry before race day.

Most road races are in the 8-kilometer to marathon range. Fun runs are usually 5 kilometers or less. The standard marathon distance is 26 miles, 385 yards. Ultra-marathons are not widespread but do have a certain following among runners. The Appendix lists standard road-racing distances, in English and metric equivalents.

A good race offers an accurately measured course (be suspicious if times seem incredibly fast), a well-marked course, the reading of intermediate times at appropriate mile or kilometer marks, a chance for all runners to cross the finish line and get an accurate time, and appropriate aid stations for long races. Most major races will be both TAC-sanctioned and TAC-certified. Sanctioning relates to medical, safety, timing, and insurance matters. Certification means that the course is accurately measured under TAC (The Athletics Congress) guidelines.

Fun runs are a good introduction to the world of competitive running. Open to all ages, they are informal, short (usually 2 to 4 miles), and . . . fun!

Avoid races with thousands of runners if you're looking for a fast time. But if you run for fun and enjoy the camaraderie of runners all about you, join the throngs. Most women runners will find themselves precisely in the middle of the bell-shaped curve that runners form: a few runners finishing very fast or very slow, with the majority in between, and the greatest number of runners finishing just about halfway between the fastest and the slowest. Consequently, in a race with 1,800 men, a woman who finishes in the top 10 of a field of 200 women is likely to find herself smashed into a large pack of male runners in six-hundredth place overall. She's not likely even to catch sight of other women runners or to have sufficient running room throughout the course.

Jennifer Daniell ran the Boston Marathon at approximately 7:30 per mile, yet it took her 12 minutes to get to the first-mile point because of the crush of the crowd. If you want to be able to run *your* pace from start to finish, enter a race with a smaller field. Although race timing is quite sophisticated these days, for your own interest and insurance, time yourself. Inexpensive digital wristwatches come with a stopwatch function and are a good investment for both racing and training. Only you know when you actually crossed the starting line, and since most large races extrapolate times during mass finishes, you can time yourself more accurately. You also can catch your own splits (intermediate times) more accurately and calculate your race pace once you are running unimpeded (in mega-races, usually from the mile mark on.).

Running in an all-women race is an exhilarating experience. Suddenly you get a clear idea of where you really are in the pack. For once, a woman gets to cross the finish line first, the winner of the whole race rather than "just" the winner of the women's division.

When you enter a race, you should have an idea of your approximate finish time. With the exception of races of 20 miles or longer, you should have covered the race distance in practice several times, with some idea of the amount of time it took. If you're entering a 10-mile race for the first time and know that you usually run 10 miles in 80 minutes (8:00 per mile), then your estimated finish time should be a bit faster than 80 minutes.

Some races will try to seed runners according to their estimated finish times. Cooperate with the race officials and go to the front of the area designated for your pace. (If you run 80:00 or a bit faster, you'll be trying to run 8:00 per mile.) Start the race at a comfortable speed, not much faster than you'd normally run in training. After you've raced more, you'll know more precisely what kind of pace you can handle in a race.

Some runners find it helpful to memorize or write their splits on their arms. To run an 80-minute 10-mile, you should pass the 1-mile mark in 8:00, the

2-mile mark in 16:00, the 5-mile mark in 40:00, and so on. You can almost guarantee yourself a faster time if you run evenly paced.

Do 5 to 10 minutes of easy jogging and stretching before the race starts so that you're warmed up and ready to go when the gun sounds. The most common mistake the novice runner makes is going out too fast. Be conservative; move out slowly and pick up your pace at the end of the race if you have anything left. It's more exhilarating to be passing other runners at the end of the race than to be passed yourself.

In hot weather and during long races, take in liquid as soon as it's offered. If you wait until you feel the need to drink, it's probably too late. It takes time for the liquid to get into your system. If you're drinking from paper cups, either stop and drink or fold over the edges of the cup to form a spout. If it's hot, pour any excess water on your head.

When you finish the race, make sure you cross the finish line and take part in finish procedures. There may be a chute to follow; you will probably have a pull-tag removed from your race number. (If you are not officially entered in the race, do not clutter up the finish area by coming near the finish line. Drop out of the race well before the finish line. Race crashers foul up race results, and the practice is frowned upon.) After the race, take time to jog or walk around in order to cool down properly. Get something to drink and head for the shower and clean clothes.

You will probably discover some new muscles in your first race, and running the following day may be painful. Before resuming your regular training, jog easily for a few days until the stiffness and soreness are gone.

TRACK AND CROSS-COUNTRY RACES

Finding racing opportunities in cross-country and track isn't as easy as finding a road race if you're no longer in school.

Cross-country races in the United States are run in the fall over varied terrain: on flat courses, on hilly, dusty trails, in parks, around athletic fields— wherever there's running space. Every course is different.

The standard women's cross-country distance is 5,000 to 8,000 meters (roughly 3 to 4 miles). Most cross-country races are run separately for men and women, which is good because it gives the women runners a chance to compete against each other. Schools and clubs have regularly scheduled meets, some of which are open to unattached runners as well. Check with them; you may be permitted to compete in their races, at least on an exhibition basis.

Running and racing opportunities are unlimited. You can try the challenge of long-distance relay races, such as the Hood-to-Coast relay, in Oregon, or you can try mixed sports events such as a triathlon, where contestants compete in a long-distance swim, a road run, and a bike race.

The challenging terrain and the unimportance of time make cross-country an appealing change from road races and track races. "International-style" cross-country races, featuring rugged courses with ditches, barriers, and sometimes water jumps, can make you feel like a kid again, delighting in the unexpected.

In certain areas, all-comers' track meets are held in the summer, or even year-round, and can be fun if you want to test yourself on the track. They are generally sponsored by park districts or track clubs. Check with your local newspaper for details.

High-school and college runners will have an extensive spring track schedule, but the older runner may have to do some scrounging to find meets if she's not a national-class athlete. You may be allowed to compete as an unattached runner in smaller college meets or in large invitational college meets when club teams are invited. Developmental meets, open to all athletes, are sometimes held in conjunction with major meets for national-class athletes, and some states also have well-organized schedules of open meets sponsored by TAC.

RACING TACTICS

Most women runners find the idea of racing tactics foreign to them. Yet as they ease into more racing, they may find the competitive juices flowing for the first time. Racing—really racing, in the sense of trying to beat the competition—can be fun if you don't become obsessed with it. At its best, "real" racing will bring out your best performance and give you the satisfaction of having pushed yourself to your limits.

When racing, focus on the runners of your ability. There's nothing to be gained by sprinting to the lead if you're destined to finish 5 minutes behind the leaders. Don't be sucked into a pace that's too fast. Tuck into a group of runners of your ability and let them do the work, breaking the wind for you. Run on your opponent's shoulder. When you're ready to pass her, do it with authority. Surge past her and get at least 40 or 50 meters ahead of her before you settle back into your pace. If she passes you back, sit on her again. Either test her again with another surge or wait until the final stage of the race to outkick her. Don't make your final sprint until you're confident that you can carry the increased pace all the way to the finish. Then dig in and go for it.

This gentle reminder is posted at the top of a long hill on an Oregon cross-country trail.

RACE ETIQUETTE

Miss Manners has yet to address proper etiquette in races, but that time may come. Follow pre-race instructions. Don't run unofficially. Line up with runners of your ability. Don't sprint to the lead and then fade. Don't jump in a race after it has started. Be courteous. Be friendly, but don't impose your company on others unless the feeling is obviously reciprocated. Don't offer unsolicited advice.

Does there exist a woman road racer who has not had a male runner offer her all sorts of "running tips," obviously ignorant of the fact that if they're running the same pace in a race, she's probably the superior runner, based on physiological differences? There's not much you can do when another runner latches on to you during a race and starts piling on the running tips. Be noncommittal and try to get past the offending competitor.

Pacing—that is, having a superior runner agree to set a pace for you during a race—has become an issue for women runners. In the middle or back of the pack, no one cares if a woman runner is paced by a man who might be the superior runner. Who's to say who's pacing whom? But farther up in the pack, with prize money, awards, and recognition at stake, women should make a concerted effort to run solo. There is an advantage to being paced by a runner of superior ability. Your companion can break the wind for you, get fluids and sponges for you, monitor your pace, give you encouragement, and disparage your competitors. If you consider yourself a "real" racer, however, you won't allow yourself to be paced.

OTHER RUNNING ADVENTURES

There's more besides fun runs, road races, marathons, and track and cross-country races. You can compete in triathlons (swim-bike-run), biathlons (swim-run), 24-hour relays, or two-person 10-mile relays. You can run up mountains, "ride and tie" with a horse, or race through wooded areas with a compass and a map (orienteering). You can run across your state; you can run 100 miles through wilderness. You can even run 170 kilometers through the Himalayas, at altitudes from 7,000 to 16,000 feet.

The newest events on the running scene offer sociability and adventure. Long (100- to 200-mile) relays with teams of 5 to 20 runners cover beautiful and challenging terrain, and involve detailed planning and logistics. They offer a unique setting for teamwork, camaraderie, and a new type of racing (running several hard legs with a few hours rest in between). The 170-mile Hood-to-Coast Relay in Oregon is one of the older relays of this type. The event has grown phenomenally, drawing some 400 11-runner teams in 1988. A wide variety of categories (coed teams, women's teams, corporate teams, masters' teams, etc.) offers a niche for every kind of runner. For me, a quarter-century of road races has turned into a blur of memories, but the sensation of floating downhill from Mt. Hood at 2 A.M. with only the dim light of a clouded new moon is burnished forever in my memory.

Running vacations offer another kind of adventure. You can sign up to tour Bali or Barbados, London or Scandinavia, and take in a local race. Maybe the Honolulu Marathon or Iron Man Triathlon is just the excuse you need to finally make that trip to Hawaii.

8

The Young Runner

There are few arguments against running for young girls. They will benefit in the same ways that adults do—increased cardiovascular fitness, stronger muscles, better weight control, and improved body tone. As long as a young girl plays at running, there's little potential for harm.

GROWTH PATTERNS

Until puberty, boys and girls can compete on a nearly equal basis. The biggest differences in performance are probably due to experience, not sex. Until around age 9, youngsters mature fairly evenly. Then girls make a quantum leap, growing taller, more coordinated, and heavier. But a girl's growth stops when she reaches the age of 15 or 16, while a boy continues to develop until he is 20 or 21. And, as pointed out in Chapter 4, puberty doesn't improve a woman's athletic performance as it does a man's.

Girls grow to have a significantly lower center of gravity than boys. They develop heavier thighs and wider hips, whereas boys carry their weight in their upper bodies, with broad shoulders and more muscular torsos. Although girls have a better sense of balance, boys have the mechanical and structural advantage, giving them greater speed and force.

Although maturity doesn't bless a woman with a physical advantage over her young male counterpart, she will find that age is not the predicting factor in terms of athletic performance that it is for men. You've probably seen proof in your own local races: 13-year-old girls running stride for stride with the best veteran runners. In fact, both preteen girls and women over 40 have run marathons in less than 3 hours. On the other hand, no preteen boys have run

145

Girls can compete as runners too, but their most intense years of training and competition should wait until after puberty.

Young girls' races should emphasize fun…

marathons under 2½ hours, although numerous men over 40 have. (The difference is even more dramatic in sports such as gymnastics and figure skating, where preadolescent girls compete at an elite level internationally.)

However, the girl who brings home medals at an early age does not automatically keep on improving as she matures. If a girl stays athletically active and maintains a healthy diet, she'll probably be able to avoid the "spread" that hits so many young women in high school and college. Yet she can't control the widening of her hips or certain other aspects of her growth that may make running more difficult.

One national age-group record holder for the half-mile set the world on fire as an 11- and 12-year-old, running 10 miles a day and recording times in the low 2:20s. Yet when an injury sidelined her as a ninth-grader, she was horrified to see her gangly, skinny body suddenly put on weight as she con-

. . . and friendship. Winning and competitiveness should be downplayed.

tinued to shoot up. After gaining 30 pounds and growing several inches in one year, she no longer had a runner's body—and she was never able to retrieve it, despite continued training. She gradually made the switch to field events and ended up as a powerful and well-coordinated softball and volleyball player.

Other age-group runners go through adolescence with fewer growth problems, but they may find their performances leveling out, time improvements harder to come by, and the competition getting stiffer as girls with no running background suddenly start catching up to them.

Adolescence need not be debilitating for the young female runner, but she must be prepared to deal with the changes her body will undergo.

TRAINING AND MATURATION

Physical activity is only one of many factors that may influence growth and maturation in a child. Regular physical training has no apparent effect on stature in growing youngsters, nor on skeletal maturation, writes Dr. Robert Malina, a professor of anthropology at the University of Texas. Training is, however, a significant factor in the regulation of body weight and composition and in the development of the skeletal and muscle tissues. There is some evidence that intensive training may delay the beginning of menstruation, but there is not a definite cause-and-effect sequence.

R. E. Frisch and other researchers estimate that for every year a girl trains intensely prior to menarche, the onset of menstruation will be delayed up to five months. The delay may actually be beneficial, and there is no evidence of permanent effects, such as infertility.

Delayed menarche (onset of menstruation) may reduce the risk of breast cancer, which is related to the cumulative number of ovulatory cycles. From an athletic point of view, the delay may provide an advantage in some sports by promoting tallness and thinness. There is a certain self-selection of athletes in any given sport which affects the profile of the group as a whole. Gymnastics, for example, attracts girls with delayed puberty and short stature. Swimmers, as a group, are taller than their nonathletic counterparts even before training.

Girls who start menstruating at a normal or early time may leave the sport earlier than others for two reasons, also affecting the profile of those involved. First, loss of an athletic physique may be enough for some girls to give up on a sport, especially if performance declines. Second, early-maturing girls usually find greater social involvement with nonsport groups as they begin their pubertal change. The late bloomers, on the other hand, "are more likely to find sports participation socially gratifying," says Dr. Oded Bar-Or.

Although delayed menarche generally is not a problem, girls who haven't developed secondary sex characteristics by age 14 or who have not started menstruating by 16 should see a physician for an exam and evaluation to rule out a serious condition.

Malina believes that socio-cultural changes may eventually have the greatest impact on adolescent girl athletes. Writing of the decline or relative flatness of performance curves during female adolescence, he sees a reflection of "both biologic and cultural factors, and with recent emphasis on, and opportunity for, athletic competition for young girls and wider acceptability of women in the role of an athlete, the overall age-related pattern of physical performance during female adolescence may change."

DISTANCE RUNNING

What young girls do best is distance running. The renowned German distance coach Ernst Van Aaken pointed out that healthy boys or girls should be able to run as many as 3 miles at a moderate pace, because their endurance is high. What these youngsters do badly is sprint. They lack the strength needed in sprinting, which can only come with growth. Yet a look at most track-meet schedules for young children will show an abundance of sprinting events.

Young runners have lower oxygen reserves than adults and less blood sugar for quick conversion to energy under conditions of high stress, so they can't possibly do as well as adults in efforts that rely upon maximum oxygen and carbohydrate burning. On the other hand, even untrained children have high rates of oxygen uptake, a good measure of endurance. When maximal aerobic capacity (oxygen consumption) is measured in relation to body size, children are found to have a relatively greater ability to utilize oxygen than adults.

Young girls, particularly, are likely to excel in distance events, compared with boys and adult women, because at the early ages of 12 and 13 they work

Running with your daughter, or anyone else in your family for that matter, can be one of the real pleasures of running.

most efficiently in terms of cardiac cost, a measure of stress on the heart. There is no further improvement with increasing age. On the other hand, a boy of the same age has only one third the cardiac capacity of males in the 30-to-36 age group. Similarly, the maximum oxygen consumption for females reaches a peak in 8- and 9-year-olds, declines for the next six or seven years, and then remains constant. Boys peak between 15 and 16 and maintain that level through young adulthood.

LSD running should be encouraged for the young girl runner, while fast interval training should be avoided. Faster-paced running can be introduced to the young runner in fartlek (see Chapter 7) and noncompetitive running games. Some attention to form, mechanics, and running strategy can be given at an early age, since young girls tend to overstride and approach each race the same way—running all out as long as they can before slowing to a jog, instead of running at an even pace.

Researcher A. Viru insists that, in all events, maximum racing potential is reached in the third decade. Speed develops slowly, and intensive interval training should be used only moderately before puberty; weight training should be avoided completely for the preadolescent because muscles, bones, and joints aren't sufficiently mature.

TRAINING AND RACING

Organized training sessions should be minimal for the very young runner. Running should be strictly recreational—going for a jog with Mom or Dad— with competition just for fun. Training sessions are needed only to familiarize the youngster with the basics of the competitive event—where a race starts and finishes, and how far it is. All-comers' meets and fun runs are good places to introduce a child to competition, with junior-high programs offering an appropriate second step in organized competition.

If your child is going to run in an organized road race, see that someone accompanies her. A five- or six-year-old has no place in a distance race unless she's accompanied by an adult. Children that young can't be expected to know the course and are vulnerable to vicious dogs or careless drivers, who often can't see racers shorter than four feet. Even if the race is on a closed-to-traffic course, your child shouldn't be unattended. Children are also less able to deal with heat than adults and should be encouraged to drink plenty of fluids. A watchful adult companion should be alert to early signs of heat distress in a young runner (see Chapter 6). If your child is struggling, don't hesitate to enjoin her to slow down, walk, rest, or even drop out. Remember, running should be fun.

Too many parents think it's "cute" to enter their tots in races. They don't bother to find out if the child has any interest in the event. Childhood should be a time of introduction to a variety of sports. Let your child take part in as many as she wishes and encourage her to watch competitive events, to see if she might like to try one. Don't push her into one sport and demand that she stick with it, train hard, and produce results.

The desire for success and recognition is a part of all of us, yet many parents look to their children for that kind of ego gratification. Too often the child's interests and needs are overlooked. When Mom and Dad invest a lot of time and money to make Sally a track star, it becomes difficult for Sally to lose or to say, "I want to quit."

If a child does decide to make a commitment to a sport, by joining a local track club, for instance, make sure she realizes that her commitment is to attend practices regularly and follow team rules, not to become number one. As a parent, it's imperative that you keep success and failure in the background, so that the child does not conclude that parental love depends on her athletic achievements.

When children are young, it's easy for them to succeed in sports by training, simply because most of their competitors are untrained or are less physically advanced. Adolescence is the great leveler, and as more children start to train for sports such as track, the chances of an individual's being a consistent winner diminish.

Many parents seem to forget that their children are indeed children. Why should a child of five, six, seven, or eight have to deal with sports in terms of individual dedication? Dedication is difficult enough for an adult athlete. A young child should learn about sports, play with sports, have fun with sports— not develop a do-or-die dedication to sports.

There is a huge attrition rate in age-group runners. Don McIntyre, of the Golden Spikes Track Club, reported a quit-rate of 80 percent for his team. Dr. Harmon Brown, an endocrinologist long active with girls' track programs, traced the progress among young runners competing in the California state cross-country meet and found a dropout rate of about 50 percent per year. After the first three years, only 15 percent of the original group remained.

"I think that we must take a hard look at our program as it is presently organized," said Brown, "and realize that participation in the nine-and-under and ten-to-eleven age groups is not (I emphasize *not*) the great spawning ground for our girl's and women's programs that we have supposed it to be, or as it is purported to be in age-group swimming."

Brown pointed out that although the dropout rate is higher among lower-ranked runners, the best are not immune, "so that the attrition can't be blamed entirely on survival of the fittest."

The world-record holders of today were not age-group-record holders as elementary school children. In most cases, they weren't even competing in track that early. A child should be allowed to find pleasure in her successes in the present. There's no need to burden her with predictions of Olympic medals, or to imply that she must continue with the sport at all costs until she reaches some predetermined goal set by her parents.

Running itself is unlikely to harm a young girl; neither will healthy competition. But steer clear of the high-pressure age-group programs that focus on intense training, national championships, and age-group records. The pressures of big-time competition are difficult enough for college-age runners. As a parent, keep your involvement in your child's program minimal. You may be called upon to transport kids or hold a stopwatch at a meet, but you're not the one to coach your daughter. A child's sports activity should not take over a whole household—with Dad the coach, Mom the driver, and every weekend spent hauling kids to meets across the country or raising money to fly 10-year-olds to a national championship half a continent away.

Preteen-age runners can be given the chance to sample competitive running in a low-key setting with the emphasis on fun running, not serious training. The junior-high-age runner may show promise of brilliance—it's not uncommon for eighth- and ninth-grade girls to outrun their eleventh- and twelfth-grade counterparts—but hold the reins a bit. The junior-high runner can be encouraged to compete in her school program and perhaps in events held on a regional basis. Resist the temptation to let her enter every race she can find because she's currently on top. Resist the temptation to let her "find out just how good she can be" at that age.

For the junior-high girl, growth and development are more important than setting age-group records. With increasing evidence of amenorrhea and eating disorders among young runners, it's imperative to deal sensitively with these athletes. Dr. Nathan Smith writes in *Kidsports* that it is "not uncommon to encounter a young high school girl who is hiding from normal maturing opportunities and responsibilities in her intense commitment to a sport program. . . . [She] lets commitment get out of hand . . . with miles of running." The inevitable result, he believes, is weight loss, confusion, depression, and deterioration of what perhaps never was truly outstanding sport performance.

Watch for signs of obsessive/compulsive behavior among young runners. Prompt control of athletic activities and counseling may be necessary. Let your

If mom says it's fun,
it must be.

daughter train wisely and compete on her appropriate level, but keep the sport in perspective and help her realize that she should wait until after puberty for her most intense years of training and competition.

When she reaches high school, a young female runner may face a dilemma. Although high-school programs for girls are standard in most areas, the truly talented high-school runner may have to search out a club team for better competition and coaching. As a result she may be faced with a choice between school and club competition. Some schools allow both, others don't. A handful of high-school-age girls can and do compete on a national level, and that kind of competition can be made available for the qualified runner.

With luck, the high-school runner will retain her enthusiasm, because her best years lie ahead in college running and beyond. The lure of athletic scholarships will keep some girls motivated, but the cautious college coach, when recruiting, is more likely to go after the girl with good marks who has been competing for only a few years with steady signs of improvement. Few college coaches are willing to offer scholarships to girls who set age-group records at 12 or 13 but who haven't advanced since. Women's collegiate competition is

From fun runs to national invitationals, distance races are open to girls.

well established, and the collegiate runner has a good chance to benefit from the coaching and successful training programs that have boosted U.S. showings in international track competition.

YOUTH RUNNING PROGRAMS

We've addressed the issue of too much running for children, but the country's greatest problem is lack of activity in the young set. Only one state (Illinois) requires physical education every day for all students. California public schools no longer require PE for graduation. Studies show that, for the first time, the present generation of youth is less fit than their parents. If you check the number of under-20 entries in a local road race, you'll find few.

A number of cities, including Spokane, Washington, and Davenport, Iowa, have developed comprehensive running-based fitness programs, coordinated by local running organizations and school systems. The programs culminate with a festive race and a strong emphasis on participation rather than performance.

The Memorial Medical Center of Long Beach, California, offers a model program that lasts 10 weeks and operates three days per week. Kids learn about stretching, warming up, running, and cooling down. Each training session includes 15 to 20 minutes of walking/jogging/running. The children gradually progress from mostly walking to continuous running. Some 1,500 children ran in the culminating race the first year; 4,000 ran the second year.

Even if there are no organized running programs for children in your area, you can take steps to encourage fitness in general:

- Turn off the TV set.
- Give your child unstructured play time in an environment that allows for physical activity (at a playground, in a gym, in your yard).
- Organize family excursions that center on physical activity, such as hiking, biking, canoeing.
- Expose your child to a variety of sports; let her choose her favorite.
- Don't use the car for short trips; walk with your children.
- Emphasize self-improvement, not competitive success.
- Encourage your child to play games that involve movement.
- Emphasize fun, not "training."
- Help your child set realistic goals in the sport of her choice.
- Don't try to compete vicariously through your child.
- Be a role model. Let your child see that you enjoy sports.

It's only natural that a running mom wants to see her child try running too. There's a healthy trend towards having kids' races (usually 1 to 3 kilometers) in conjunction with longer road races. These noncompetitive fun runs are the perfect way to let your child sample road racing. They're short enough that a child should be able to run, jog, or walk the distance without having trained for it. Let your child experience the thrill of meeting a challenge. A warm hug and words of praise will go a long way.

9

The Golden Years of Running

My generation grew up with the vision of plump, rosy-cheeked grandmothers holding open the kitchen door for the grandkids with one hand, carrying a hot pan of fresh-from-the-oven cookies in the other. Grandma still may have rosy cheeks these days, but they just as likely came from a 2-mile jog through the neighborhood as from working in a hot kitchen.

Take 65-year-old Helen Klein. Four kids, seven grandchildren, three great-grandchildren. Her idea of a summer vacation is running four 100-mile races in a four-month period. Oh, and not just any old 100-milers, but mountainous ones involving trail-running at high altitude.

Klein, a retired nurse, took up running in her fifties, deciding she "didn't want to just play bridge, eat candy, and go to pot."

She confessed to being embarrassed "to go out in public in those skimpy running clothes. My mother had always told me girls should never sweat. She would say, 'Horses sweat.'" Her husband built a ⅕-mile grass running track around their yard and she took her first laps there, nearly passing out on a hot and humid day. Responding to prodding from a running friend, Klein stuck with her jogging and was up to a non-stop mile in a week. Each week she added a mile and was up to a 10-mile run in 10 weeks. She entered a 10-miler, won her age group, took home a trophy, and was hooked. She moved up to marathons in a few years, then on to 50-milers, 100-milers, and even a 280-mile five-day race.

Klein's accomplishments may be extraordinary, but her late entry into running isn't.

Masters (over 40) running is the fastest-growing part of the sport, and women—largely because of their lack of running history—have made some of the biggest news in the field. A national TV audience was watching when

157

You don't have to be a teenager to become a runner, as these mature competitors demonstrate.

42-year-old Priscilla Welch was the first woman to cross the finish line in the 1987 New York City Marathon, the same year she set Great Britain's national record (and a world masters record) of 2:26:51 in the London Marathon. And this from a former smoker who ran her first marathon in 1980, clocking a modest 3:26. TV viewers saw her again in 1988 during the Seoul Olympics coverage. This time she was running in national ads for Nike, exhorting us all to "Just do it!"

Or consider the feats of Sister Marion Irvine, the running nun from Sacramento who ran with the middle of the pack in the first-ever U.S. Women's Olympic Marathon Trial in 1984. At age 54, she ran 2:52:02.

In 1987 more than 1,000 women, aged 35 to 80-plus, paid their way to Melbourne, Australia, to compete in the VII World Veterans' Games. They came from at least three dozen countries to take part in a wide range of track and field events, from 100 meters to the marathon, from the high jump to the hammer throw. The events offered for men and women were identical. The women represented close to 20 percent of the 5,000 athletes who gathered for the Games.

Masters running has grown to the extent that half the runners in the Boston Marathon are 40 or older. This growth attests to the true nature of running—that of a lifelong sport. The running "boomers" are graying, no question about that, but they're still running and they're adding to their numbers. Senior sports are expanding on all fronts, and senior fitness may well be the next sport industry to hit the big time as our older population increases in proportion to the younger folk.

In the past decade, research on women runners has filled many knowledge gaps. Senior fitness is the next avenue to be fully explored. How does aging affect athletic performance? How does menopause affect a female athlete? How hard should we push ourselves as we grow older? What are the warning signs that tell us to cut back?

The pioneers of women's masters running—the likes of Ruth Anderson, Mavis Lindgren, Miki Gorman, and Marcie Trent—opened eyes and doors for thousands of others. They showed that a woman with no running history could embark on the sport at any time—in her thirties or her sixties—and find success, and they paved the way for two groups of women runners to find their way to masters competition: They showed the need for age-group divisions and records, so that the late-blooming jogger cum racer could feel comfortable competing at her own level, and so that runners such as former record-setters Doris Brown Heritage, Joyce Smith, and Jacqueline Hansen could keep on competing and get the recognition they deserved.

How good can masters women be? (At present a 35-year-old woman is eligible for international masters competition, but 40 is the more commonly accepted threshhold for masters men and women.) Women like Grete Waitz are still at the top in open competition during their mid-thirties. The question is, how many will still be racing seriously when they're in their forties? Heritage is still the only over-40 runner to break 5:00 for the mile, although Welch and Smith are probably capable of doing so (at age 46, Smith was the eleventh-place finisher in the 1984 Olympic Marathon).

Masters women are enjoying a golden decade, holding their own against women half their age. A smaller pool of runners (compared to men) opens the way for an elite masters woman to challenge open competitors. Yet the most important reason for the athletic success of these "older" women may be psychological, argues Jack Daniels.

"There are only so many years you feel enthusiastic about something," he explains. For pre–Title IX women whose only athletic options were cheerleading or Girls Athletic Association playdays, the fires of enthusiasm are just igniting. Many women, competitive by nature, are finding an athletic outlet for the first time. They're also finding that there are few limits in their part of the sport because so few have been around to set them.

Daniels says that there are no great differences between men and women when it comes to aging and its effects on fitness. Yet the fact that the fastest open male runners have yet to become masters record-holders suggest two truths about high-intensity training and competition: Your mind and body can take only so much. If one doesn't go, the other will.

Injuries may curtail a running career. For others, competitive goals may already have been achieved. (After an Olympic gold medal, what does Frank Shorter really have to prove?) For many, other activities, such as work and family, must take priority over intense training.

Daniels believes that a runner's competitive career has to be limited by how hard the runner has worked over the years: "Some people have long careers of success, some short. The ones with short careers realized their potential when they were young—at their peak years. The ones who were good for a long time, say at 25, 30, and 35, weren't running to their potential during their prime years but were able to maintain their performance by realizing a greater percentage of their potential while that absolute potential was lowering because of age."

The runner who continues her hard training on into "masterhood" will gradually find her PR days growing more distant. Yet the runner who takes up the sport at a later age may surprise herself by running faster even as her body is slowing down. Running experts variously give a runner 7 to 10 years to realize her competitive potential. For most lifelong runners, however, running competitively and setting PRs is secondary to running itself.

RUNNING AND AGING

Through running you can drastically change your body profile. To some extent, you can even avoid problems associated with aging. While aging inevitably must have a negative effect on running performance, more importantly, running can have a positive effect on you.

The older woman who wants to start running should first get medical clearance from her doctor. She also should take her first steps through a reputable jogging or running program, such as those offered by YMCAs or universities. It's particularly important for the older runner to have someone available for advice and to keep an eye out for the overexuberance of a first-time runner who may try to do too much too soon. Remember that the benefits of exercise rarely occur before 10 weeks of training.

Drs. Michael Pollack and Henry Miller of Wake Forest University report that many studies show that the deteriorating effects of sedentary living can be reversed with endurance training, although it is not yet known to what extent endurance training can reverse the deteriorating effects of aging. Their study of 26 male champion American runners from 40 to 75 years of age showed that all had excellent cardiopulmonary function and body-composition characteristics. The subjects' resulting heart rates, body fat, and serum triglycerides (fats in body fluid) were much lower than in the sedentary population, while blood pressure and serum cholesterol were about the same. One would expect a study of older women runners to show much the same thing.

Pollack concluded that "life need not be a ride down what is called the aging curve." Aging isn't going to make a huge difference in what you can run, perhaps only 10 seconds a mile over 10 years. The key is maintaining training intensity. Those runners who eased up on their training suffered the same 9 percent loss of aerobic capacity per decade that most sedentary people experience. There was, however, an important residual payoff from all the years of running, since the active people had a higher aerobic capacity to begin with than did their sedentary counterparts.

The aging process will eventually limit the amount and type of training one can adjust to, but then an athlete of any age must program her training in accordance with how her body adapts to training stimuli. In *The Complete*

Runner, Pollack and Miller note, "We all have a point at which training becomes straining. When the straining stage is reached, athletes experience a regression in performance and/or become candidates for an orthopedic disorder.

"In our experience with masters-age runners, intensity (speed) and duration (mileage) of training are the two big problem areas. As one gets older, and in the case of most of the masters runners who have had many years of sedentary living prior to resumption of training, the joints do not adapt as well to speed work or marathon training. Variability as to what type and how much training one can adapt to is quite wide. Thus training regimens should be adopted on an individual basis," they conclude. You may find your recovery time slowing down over the years. Consider cutting back on your running or alternating it with other activities.

Evidence is becoming clearer and clearer that exercise plays an important role in our health as we age. Dr. Morris Notelovitz, founder of Midlife Centers of America, writes that exercising women have a cardioprotective effect of one decade when compared to sedentary women. Regular long-term physical activity can improve "good" cholesterol (HDL) levels and max VO_2 levels in older women.

The observed decline in max VO_2 with age "probably reflects a loss of functional capacity due both to a natural age-related deterioration and to a decrease in physical activity," points out Notelovitz. "The age-associated reduction in cardiorespiratory efficiency at submaximal exercise, however, is due primarily to weight gain, rather than actual systems degeneration. The rate of decline is slower in physically active men and women."

MENOPAUSE

Menopause won't have an effect on your cardiorespiratory fitness, but your running may have a profound effect on problems normally associated with menopause.

Osteoporosis, as discussed in Chapter 5, is common in postmenopausal women and leads to repeated fractures. Estrogen treatment and adequate calcium intake (lifelong) help curb osteoporosis. Weight-bearing exercise, ideally started before menopause for maximum benefit, helps increase bone density. The greater bone-mineral mass you have at menopause, the more you can afford to lose. Exercise after menopause will help slow bone loss, which can range up to 8 percent per decade after menopause. One study showed older runners with

Priscilla Welch, who quit smoking and took up running at the age of 36, showed a late-bloomer's mettle by winning the New York Marathon in 1987.

40 percent higher bone density than sedentary women of their age.

Exercise is known to induce a state of well-being, and for a woman going through menopause it appears to reduce symptoms of depression and anxiety.

"One of the most distressing symptoms expressed by menopausal women is anxiety," notes Notelovitz. "Vigorous physical activity reduces muscle tension and is also associated with a significant decrease in anxiety. . . . [The] effect [was] noted only when the exercise was intense."

Exercise also may help another problem of menopause: insomnia. Reaction time may be better in exercisers, too; generalized rather than specific exercise appears to be the factor. Runners, for example, have improved reactive speed in their fingers.

Jean Irvin, who at age 56 has two decades of running behind her, reports "no major change" in her running caused by menopause. She goes along with the theory that running is a psychological boost for a menopausal woman, saying that "people who run are kind of optimistic anyhow."

You don't have to be a Helen Klein or Priscilla Welch to benefit from running. It's never too late to start (with medical clearance), and a 30-minute run three times a week will be adequate.

As Dr. Mona Shangold concludes, it has been well documented that exercise modifies or retards aspects of the aging process. It slows normal age-related declines in peak performance and maximal aerobic capacity. It retards loss of muscle and bone mass and the increase in body fat.

"The exercising older woman," writes Shangold, "has an aerobic capacity and body composition similar to those of much younger, sedentary women. It has been suggested that the rate of decline in many physiologic parameters may be reduced by approximately 50 percent in physically fit as compared with sedentary women."

Live longer! Feel better! Look better!

Just do it.

10

Keeping Running in Perspective

Running is not the magic elixir that some wish it to be.

Finding the motivation for it is the greatest problem most individuals face, but once you are hooked, other problems may arise. The biggest one, besides injuries, is likely to be dealing with the nonrunning world.

It's easy to let running run your life. Your friends are runners. Your social life revolves around races; your free hours and mealtimes are scheduled according to training sessions; your closet has 1 pair of street shoes and 10 pairs of running shoes; you've become a walking advertisement for every company that ever sponsored a race; you've become disenchanted with people who don't run. You may even have become the running bore who descends on runner and nonrunner alike with endless tales of your last race, current injuries, and latest miracle diet.

Life isn't easy for the nonrunner who lives with a runner. In the past it was typically the nonrunning wife who indulged her running husband's whims. What happens when the wife is the runner and the husband is not? And what happens when the wife joins her running husband and beats him in races?

One successful long-distance runner reported:

> When I started running my husband was amused, tolerant, and even a bit proud. Then I began to outrun his male friends in training—then I obviously began to outrun him. He began to feel threatened—he's a jock, I'm supposed to be the intellectual cream puff, nonathletic! He became very negative, objected to my going off to races (which equaled neglecting the family, he told me), running camps, etc. I used to win first woman award all the time—but never mentioned it to him and he never asked. As running became more

Running can be a unifying force in your family and the social event of your day.

OK, you've got young kids. But that doesn't mean they can't play in the long-jump pit while you run laps at the local track.

important to me, I felt we were heading for divorce, rapidly—though I hated the idea.

About a year ago he realized how close we were to splitting, decided to try to understand my running—came to races, met runners, ran more himself, went to occasional social gatherings and running camps. It is no longer necessary for me to keep mum about having gone out running, though I don't bring up the subject unless I'm asked. It's sort of a truce situation.

Running can enhance a marriage, however, and in some cases help cement an already positive relationship. One woman, the wife of a national-class runner, noted that since she has become a runner herself, she can better understand her husband's needs and involvement in the sport. More important, she said, her own feelings of self-worth helped her marriage. "Any time an individual feels better about herself, there's going to be more loving and giving in a relationship."

Nola Marshall surveyed Australian women runners and discovered that if a wife and husband ran together and were mutually involved in the sport, then family life was happy and the personal relationship fairly harmonious. The most important benefit from running together was discussing mutual interests. "They would talk and share each other's successes and failures and, through these highs and lows, come to understand better how their spouse was feeling, and consequently came closer together," explained Marshall.

One of the not-so-obvious benefits of running, which is often portrayed as a lonely endeavor, is that it can be the social highlight of your day. Somehow, with a few shared miles behind you, the need for small talk diminishes and you can enjoy an open, wide-ranging conversation with your running partner. The therapeutic benefits of having an attentive and sympathetic running partner as a sounding board are not to be underestimated.

Running can be a unifying force in the family, but it's important to low-key the "family that runs together . . . " theme. Remember that there are many enjoyable ways to attain fitness. Don't force your choice on other family members. Providing subtle encouragement and opportunities to run is one thing; badgering a child or spouse into running is something else. Let your own enthusiasm for running be contagious. Use a road race or out-of-town training run as an excuse for a family outing to explore new places. Involve your family as much as possible. Most important, respect your family's need for you in your role of mother and/or wife.

As your running progresses, changes are bound to occur, both in your own outlook and in the way others view you. According to one New England runner, "My mother thought running was a fad and has taken two years to accept it. My sister and brother-in-law were embarrassed by the way I looked in running clothes but are proud of me now that I have local 'fame.' Neighbors and fellow teachers who were apathetic until I got coverage in the papers are now supporting. It was initially all negative, but the longer I've done it and the better I get, the more people seem to be enthusiastic. It was hell at first!"

Running will make many positive changes in your life, but those changes may upset the status quo. You may suddenly discover that you'd rather hike or go on a two-day bike trip than play bridge in a smoke-filled room. A three-hour run on Sunday may sound better to you than packing the family into the station wagon for an all-day outing. And after a hard workout, you may prefer to throw together an unimpressive meal than spend an hour over the stove.

A lot of women have successfully integrated running into their normal daily routines without upsetting the lives of those around them. Some trade baby-sitting hours with other running mothers. Parents may take turns watching the kids while the spouse goes for a run. And in some cases, the upside-down schedule of a running household is considered normal anyway.

In my survey of women runners (see Chapter 4), 96 percent of the married women said their husbands were also runners. Many were encouraged by their husbands to start running and continue to receive encouragement. Eighty-two percent of the women felt that their immediate families (husband and children) were supportive.

Even in terms of their own personal habits, runners often have to make adjustments. Some women who have made a commitment to running simply learn to stretch their day. One sub-3:00 marathoner admitted, "I have to get up at 5:15 A.M. daily in order to get in my 10 miles of running, so I can get home in time to get the family up and off. If I leave it until late in the day, things come up that conflict with my schedule. Because I have a preschooler, I must run when my husband is home to baby-sit."

Another marathoner solved her time squeeze by running to and from work (9 miles round trip).

A New Jersey runner reported that she and her husband often "do not go to friends or to New York for theater because of my running schedule and my refusal to miss a day. Our friends must be used to the idea that I will run around their neighborhood before sitting down to dinner (not to mention using the host's bath)."

Despite the daily problems that running creates, these women have chosen to continue running. For them the rewards outweigh the problems. Most considered fitness the main reward of running. Almost half listed friendship as another highly valued reward. The majority said that running helped them emotionally and gave them a sense of well-being and self-worth.

One spoke of the "joy of discovering, knowing, and using my body; a clear head after runs; good people; solitude; a sense of 'Yes, I can.' "

And nearly all placed running high on their list of priorities, considering it as important as eating and sleeping.

"Running is very important," wrote an Indiana runner, "probably below

Whether you live at the beach, in the mountains, or on New York's Upper East Side, your environment shapes your running experience.

only my family and job/career, but part of these as well. I don't think I could be as successful at either of these without the confidence and outlet of running."

"Running blends into the other values which make up the disciplined.part of my life," wrote a Californian in her early thirties.

The happiest, and not coincidentally most successful, runners are those who've found the right balance in their lives. Running is important, yes, but it doesn't dominate life to the exclusion of all else. Running should enhance and complement your life, giving you the vigor to experience its richness.

An Olympic marathoner himself, Kenny Moore wrote of Ingrid Kristiansen, Grete Waitz, and Joan Benoit Samuelson: "Inevitably, those best at the marathon, this event that defines lasting it out, lead lives of balance. They have outlasted runners of comparable talent who destroyed it one way or another, through overtraining, overracing, dumb tactics or perfectionist burnout."

Like a marathoner, the lifelong runner must learn how to pace herself.

Here is how a buoyant masters-age competitor summed up her feelings, reflecting those of many other women:

> The unbelievable feeling of good health and stamina is reward enough, but the wonderful people we have met while running and competing are the real extra.
>
> Running has become such an important part of both my husband's and my life that when deprived of a single day of it we feel the loss. It really is more than just exercise and physical benefits, [it's] the marvelous mental escape that comes while running that is so necessary in these stressful times.

Whatever the motivation—for health or competition, for friendship or self-discovery—women are finding running a rewarding, self-enriching part of their lives. Whatever your reasons for running—and they may change from time to time—you'll find that this simple act of movement can be a glowing force in your personal growth. You deserve to be proud.

Appendix

RUNNING ORGANIZATIONS AND GOVERNING BODIES

Achilles Track Club, 356 West 34th St., New York, NY 10001, is a club for the physically disabled, with chapters around the world.

Association for Road Racing Athletes (ARRA), 1081 Paulsen Bldg., Spokane, WA 99201, deals with professional (prize-money) road racers.

The Athletics Congress (TAC), P.O. Box 120, Indianapolis, IN 46206, is the United States' national governing body for athletics (track and field, race walking, and long-distance running).

International Amateur Athletic Federation (IAAF), 3, Hans Crescent, Knightsbridge, London SW1X OLN, England, is the international governing body for athletics (track and field, race walking, and long-distance running).

International Olympic Committee (IOC), Chateau de Vidy, Ch-1107, Lausanne, Switzerland, organizes the Olympic movement and is the umbrella organization for sports federations like the IAAF.

National Association of Intercollegiate Athletics (NAIA), 1221 Baltimore, Kansas City, MO 64105, governs intercollegiate sports, including track and field, at certain U.S. universities and colleges.

National Collegiate Athletic Association (NCAA), P.O. Box 1906, Mission, KS 66201, is the largest organization governing collegiate sports in the U.S.

Road Runners Club of America (RRCA), 629 South Washington St., Alexandria, VA 22314, is the umbrella organization for hundreds of local running clubs across the U.S.

TACSTATS, 7745 Southwest 138th Terrace, Miami, FL 33158, is a TAC organization responsible for road-race age-group record keeping.

United States Olympic Committee (USOC), 1750 E. Boulder St., Colorado Springs, CO 80909-5760, is a member of the IOC and coordinates Olympic activities for various national sports federations, including TAC.

PUBLICATIONS OF INTEREST

Bowerman, W. J., and W. E. Harris, *Jogging*. New York: Grosset & Dunlap, 1967.

Clark, Nancy, *The Athlete's Kitchen: A Nutrition Guide and Cookbook*. Boston: CBI Publishing, 1981.

Cooper, Mildred and Kenneth, *Aerobics for Women*. New York: M. Evans, 1972.

Costill, David L., *A Scientific Approach to Distance Running*. Los Altos, CA: Tafnews Press, 1978.

Daniels, Jack, and Jimmy Gilbert, *Performance Tables for Distance Runners*. Oxygen Power, P.O. Box 26287, Tempe, AZ 85282. Offers detailed tables that allow you to estimate your maximum oxygen consumption based on your past performances at almost any running distance, and to project your time at other distances.

Doherty, J. Kenneth, *Track and Field Omnibook*. Los Altos, CA: Tafnews Press, 1976.

Foreman, Kenneth E., and Virginia M. Husted, *Track and Field Techniques for Girls and Women*. Dubuque, IA: William C. Brown, 1977.

Glover, Bob, and Pete Schuder, *The New Competitive Runner's Handbook*. New York: Penguin Books, 1988.

Henderson, Joe, *Joe Henderson's Running Handbook*. Dubuque, IA: William C. Brown, 1985.

Shangold, Mona, and Gabe Mirkin, *Women and Exercise: Physiology and Sports Medicine*. Philadelphia: F. A. Davis Co., 1988.

Sheehan, George A., *Medical Advice for Runners*. Mountain View, CA: Anderson/World, 1978.

RUNNING AND TRACK PERIODICALS

Athletics (1220 Sheppard Ave. E., Willowdale, Ontario M2K 2X1, Canada) is a Canadian track and field magazine which covers some long-distance races.

Joe Henderson's Running Commentary (441 Brookside, Eugene, OR 97504) is a monthly newsletter focusing on long-distance running—the latest inside news and research developments.

National Masters News (P.O. Box 2372, Van Nuys, CA 91404) offers complete coverage of track and field and distance running for masters athletes.

Road Race Management (507 2nd St. N.E., Washington, D.C. 20002) is a valuable source of information for road-race directors, elite runners, and those involved with the business or technical side of road running.

Runner's World (Rodale Press, 33 East Minor St., Emmaus, PA, 18908) is aimed at beginning and long-distance runners.

Running and FitNews (American Running and Fitness Association, 9310 Old Georgetown Rd., Bethesda, MD 20814) is a monthly newsletter with research updates on training, nutrition, injuries, and other sports-related topics.

Running Research News (P.O. Box 27041, Lansing, MI 48909) summarizes new research on running-related subjects.

Running Stats (1085 14th St., Suite 1260, Boulder, CO 80302) provides the quickest access to national and international road-race results.

Running Times (P.O. Box 6509, Syracuse, NY 13217-6509) covers U.S. road racing and carries an extensive race calendar.

Track and Field News (Box 296, Los Altos, CA 94022) reports on international track and field events and some road racing.

Ultrarunning (300 N. Main St., P.O. Box 481, Sunderland, MA 01375) covers races longer than the marathon.

Women's Sports and Fitness (World Publications, Inc., 809 S. Orlando Ave., Suite H, Winter Park, FL 32789) is a glossy national magazine devoted to a variety of women's sports and fitness subjects, but with a major emphasis on running.

HELPFUL ORGANIZATIONS

American Dietetic Association, 430 N. Michigan Ave., Chicago, IL 60611, provides nutrition information, including food exchange lists for meal planning.

Anorexia Nervosa and Related Eating Disorders (ANRED), P.O. Box 5102, Eugene, OR 97405.

Melpomene Institute for Women's Health Research, 2125 East Hennepin Ave., Minneapolis, MN 55413, offers a newsletter, brochures, and packets of research information; instigates research on women's health and fitness issues, including exercise during pregnancy, osteoporosis, body image, and children's sports.

National Association of Anorexia Nervosa and Associated Disorders (ANAD), P.O. Box 271, Highland Park, IL 60035.

METERS/ENGLISH DISTANCE EQUIVALENTS

100 meters = 109 yards, 1 foot, 1 inch
200 meters = 218 yards, 2 feet, 2 inches
400 meters = 437 yards, 1 foot, 4 inches
800 meters = 874 yards, 2 feet, 8 inches
1000 meters = 1093 yards, 1 foot, 10 inches
1500 meters = 1640 yards, 1 foot, 3 inches
3000 meters = 1 mile, 1520 yards, 2 feet, 6 inches
5000 meters = 3 miles, 188 yards, 2.4 inches
10,000 meters = 6 miles, 376 yards, 4.8 inches

100 yards = 91.44 meters
220 yards = 201.168 meters
440 yards = 402.336 meters
880 yards = 804.672 meters
1 mile = 1609.344 meters
2 miles = 3218.688 meters
3 miles = 4828.032 meters
6 miles = 9656.064 meters

KILOMETER/MILE EQUIVALENTS

1 kilometer = .62 miles
1.5 kilometers = .93 miles
2 kilometers = 1.24 miles
3 kilometers = 1.86 miles
5 kilometers = 3.11 miles
8 kilometers = 4.97 miles
10 kilometers = 6.21 miles
15 kilometers = 9.32 miles
20 kilometers = 12.43 miles
25 kilometers = 15.54 miles
30 kilometers = 18.64 miles
50 kilometers = 31.07 miles
100 kilometers = 62.14 miles

Marathon = 42.195 kilometers = 26.22 miles

EVENT DIFFERENTIALS

100 yards to 100 meters: multiply your time by 1.09
   (11.0 for 100 yards = 11.99 for 100 meters)
220 yards to 200 meters: multiply by .994
   (25.0 for 220 yards = 24.85 for 200 meters)
440 yards to 400 meters: multiply by .994
   (60.0 for 440 yards = 59.64 for 400 meters)
880 yards to 800 meters: multiply by .994
   (2:25.0 for 880 yards = 2:24.2 for 800 meters)
Mile to 1500 meters: multiply by .926
   (5:00.0 for the mile = 4:37.8 for 1500 meters)
3 miles to 5000 meters: multiply by 1.036
   (18:00.0 for 3 miles = 18:38.9 for 5000 meters)
6 miles to 10,000 meters: multiply by 1.036
   (36:00.0 for 6 miles = 37:17.8 for 10,000 meters)

Note: To convert from metric events to times for English events, divide by the appropriate number.

PACING TABLES

Track Races (1 Lap = 440 Yards)*

LAP	SECONDS PER LAP																	
	65	66	67	68	69	70	71	72	73	74	75	76	77	78	79	80	81	82
2	2:10	2:12	2:14	2:16	2:18	2:20	2:22	2:24	2:26	2:28	2:30	2:32	2:34	2:36	2:38	2:40	2:42	2:44
3	3:15	3:18	3:21	3:24	3:27	3:30	3:33	3:36	3:39	3:42	3:45	3:48	3:51	3:54	3:57	4:00	4:03	4:06
4	4:20	4:24	4:28	4:32	4:36	4:40	4:44	4:48	4:52	4:56	5:00	5:04	5:08	5:12	5:16	5:20	5:24	5:28
5	5:25	5:30	5:35	5:40	5:45	5:50	5:55	6:00	6:05	6:10	6:15	6:20	6:25	6:30	6:35	6:40	6:45	6:50
6	6:30	6:36	6:42	6:48	6:54	7:00	7:06	7:12	7:18	7:24	7:30	7:36	7:42	7:48	7:54	8:00	8:06	8:12
7	7:35	7:42	7:49	7:56	8:03	8:10	8:17	8:24	8:31	8:38	8:45	8:52	8:59	9:06	9:13	9:20	9:27	9:34
8	8:40	8:48	8:56	9:04	9:12	9:20	9:28	9:36	9:44	9:52	10:00	10:08	10:16	10:24	10:32	10:40	10:48	10:56
9	9:45	9:54	10:03	10:12	10:21	10:30	10:39	10:48	10:57	11:06	11:15	11:24	11:33	11:42	11:51	12:00	12:09	12:18
10	10:50	11:00	11:10	11:20	11:30	11:40	11:50	12:00	12:10	12:20	12:30	12:40	12:50	13:00	13:10	13:20	13:30	13:40
11	11:55	12:06	12:17	12:28	12:39	12:50	13:01	13:12	13:23	13:34	13:45	13:56	14:07	14:18	14:29	14:40	14:51	15:02
12	13:00	13:12	13:24	13:36	13:48	14:00	14:12	14:24	14:36	14:48	15:00	15:12	15:24	15:36	15:48	16:00	16:12	16:24

LAP	83	84	85	86	87	88	89	90	91	92	93	94	95	96	97	98	99	100
2	2:46	2:48	2:50	2:52	2:54	2:56	2:58	3:00	3:02	3:04	3:06	3:08	3:10	3:12	3:14	3:16	3:18	3:20
3	4:09	4:12	4:15	4:18	4:21	4:24	4:27	4:30	4:33	4:36	4:39	4:42	4:45	4:48	4:51	4:54	4:57	5:00
4	5:32	5:36	5:40	5:44	5:48	5:52	5:56	6:00	6:04	6:08	6:12	6:16	6:20	6:24	6:28	6:32	6:36	6:40
5	6:55	7:00	7:05	7:10	7:15	7:20	7:25	7:30	7:35	7:40	7:45	7:50	7:55	8:00	8:05	8:10	8:15	8:20
6	8:18	8:24	8:30	8:36	8:42	8:48	8:54	9:00	9:06	9:12	9:18	9:24	9:30	9:36	9:42	9:48	9:54	10:00
7	9:41	9:48	9:55	10:02	10:09	10:16	10:23	10:30	10:37	10:44	10:51	10:58	11:05	11:12	11:19	11:26	11:33	11:40
8	11:04	11:12	11:20	11:28	11:36	11:44	11:52	12:00	12:08	12:16	12:24	12:32	12:40	12:48	12:56	13:04	13:12	13:20
9	12:27	12:36	12:45	12:54	13:03	13:12	13:21	13:30	13:39	13:48	13:57	14:06	14:15	14:24	14:33	14:42	14:51	15:00
10	13:50	14:00	14:10	14:20	14:30	14:40	14:50	15:00	15:10	15:20	15:30	15:40	15:50	16:00	16:10	16:20	16:30	16:40
11	15:13	15:24	15:35	15:46	15:57	16:08	16:19	16:30	16:41	16:52	17:03	17:14	17:25	17:36	17:47	17:58	18:09	18:20
12	16:36	16:48	17:00	17:12	17:24	17:36	17:48	18:00	18:12	18:24	18:36	18:48	19:00	19:12	19:24	19:36	19:48	20:00

Your goal in track races is to run an even pace. If you want to run 2 miles on the track in 12:00, follow the horizontal column next to lap 8 (there are eight laps in a 2-mile race) until you find 12:00. Go up the vertical column from 12:00 to find your pace per lap and your cumulative times at the end of each lap (in this case, 90 seconds for the first lap, 3:00 for two laps, 4:30 for three laps, and so on).

*Newer tracks are generally 400 meters, approximately 8 feet short of 440 yards. Times per lap are roughly ½ second faster on the shorter track at a fast pace, 1 second at a slow pace.

MILE TO MARATHON PACING CHART

MILE PACE	5K	5 MI	10K	15 K	10 MI	20K	13.1 MI	15 MI	25K	30K	20 MI	MARATHON 26.219
4:50	15:01	24:10	30:02	45:03	48:20	1:00:04	1:03:19	1:12:30	1:15:05	1:30:06	1:36:40	2:06:44
4:51	15:04	24:15	30:08	45:12	48:30	1:00:16	1:03:32	1:12:45	1:15:20	1:30:24	1:37:00	2:07:10
4:52	15:07	24:20	30:14	45:22	48:40	1:00:29	1:03:45	1:13:00	1:15:36	1:30:44	1:37:20	2:07:36
4:53	15:10	24:25	30:21	45:31	48:50	1:00:41	1:03:58	1:13:15	1:15:51	1:31:02	1:37:40	2:08:02
4:54	15:13	24:30	30:27	45:40	49:00	1:00:54	1:04:11	1:13:20	1:16:07	1:31:20	1:38:00	2:08:28
4:55	15:17	24:35	30:33	45:50	49:10	1:01:06	1:04:24	1:13:45	1:16:23	1:31:40	1:38:20	2:08:55
4:56	15:20	24:40	30:39	45:59	49:20	1:01:19	1:04:38	1:14:00	1:16:39	1:31:58	1:38:40	2:09:21
4:57	15:23	24:45	30:45	46:08	49:30	1:01:31	1:04:51	1:14:15	1:16:54	1:32:16	1:39:00	2:09:47
4:58	15:26	24:50	30:52	46:18	49:40	1:01:43	1:05:04	1:14:30	1:17:10	1:32:36	1:39:20	2:10:13
4:59	15:29	24:55	30:58	46:27	49:50	1:01:56	1:05:17	1:14:45	1:17:25	1:32:54	1:39:40	2:10:39
5:00	15:32	25:00	31:04	46:36	50:00	1:02:08	1:05:30	1:15:00	1:17:40	1:33:12	1:40:00	2:11:06
5:01	15:35	25:05	31:10	46:45	50:10	1:02:21	1:05:43	1:15:15	1:17:56	1:33:30	1:40:20	2:11:32
5:02	15:38	25:10	31:17	46:55	50:20	1:02:33	1:05:56	1:15:30	1:18:11	1:33:50	1:40:40	2:11:58
5:03	15:41	25:15	31:23	47:04	50:30	1:02:46	1:06:09	1:15:45	1:18:27	1:34:08	1:41:00	2:12:24
5:04	15:44	25:20	31:29	47:13	50:40	1:02:58	1:06:22	1:16:00	1:18:42	1:34:26	1:41:20	2:12:51
5:05	15:48	25:25	31:35	47:23	50:50	1:03:10	1:06:36	1:16:15	1:18:58	1:34:46	1:41:40	2:13:17
5:06	15:51	25:30	31:41	47:32	51:00	1:03:23	1:06:49	1:16:30	1:19:14	1:35:04	1:42:00	2:13:43
5:07	15:54	25:35	31:48	47:41	51:10	1:03:35	1:07:02	1:16:45	1:19:29	1:35:22	1:42:20	2:14:09
5:08	15:57	25:40	31:54	47:51	51:20	1:03:48	1:07:15	1:17:00	1:19:45	1:35:42	1:42:40	2:14:35
5:09	16:00	25:45	32:00	48:00	51:30	1:04:00	1:07:28	1:17:15	1:20:00	1:36:00	1:43:00	2:15:02
5:10	16:03	25:50	32:06	48:09	51:40	1:04:13	1:07:41	1:17:30	1:20:16	1:36:18	1:43:20	2:15:28
5:11	16:06	25:55	32:12	48:19	51:50	1:04:25	1:07:54	1:17:45	1:20:31	1:36:38	1:43:40	2:15:54
5:12	16:09	26:00	32:19	48:28	52:00	1:04:37	1:08:07	1:18:00	1:20:46	1:36:56	1:44:00	2:16:20
5:13	16:12	26:05	32:25	48:37	52:10	1:04:50	1:08:20	1:18:15	1:21:02	1:37:14	1:44:20	2:16:47
5:14	16:16	26:10	32:31	48:47	52:20	1:05:02	1:08:33	1:18:30	1:21:18	1:37:34	1:44:40	2:17:13
5:15	16:19	26:15	32:37	48:56	52:30	1:05:15	1:08:47	1:18:45	1:21:34	1:37:52	1:45:00	2:17:39
5:16	16:22	26:20	32:44	49:05	52:40	1:05:27	1:09:00	1:19:00	1:21:49	1:38:10	1:45:20	2:18:05

MILE PACE	5K	5 MI	10K	15 K	10 MI	20K	13.1 MI	15 MI	25K	30K	20 MI	MARATHON 26.219
5:17	16:25	26:25	32:50	49:15	52:50	1:05:39	1:09:13	1:19:15	1:22:04	1:38:30	1:45:40	2:18:31
5:18	16:28	26:30	32:56	49:24	53:00	1:05:52	1:09:26	1:19:30	1:22:20	1:38:48	1:46:00	2:18:58
5:19	16:31	26:35	33:02	49:33	53:10	1:06:04	1:09:39	1:19:45	1:22:35	1:39:06	1:46:20	2:19:24
5:20	16:34	26:40	33:08	49:43	53:20	1:06:17	1:09:52	1:20:00	1:22:51	1:39:26	1:46:40	2:19:50
5:21	16:37	26:45	33:15	49:52	53:30	1:06:29	1:10:05	1:20:15	1:23:06	1:39:44	1:47:00	2:20:16
5:22	16:40	26:50	33:21	50:01	53:40	1:06:42	1:10:18	1:20:30	1:23:22	1:40:02	1:47:20	2:20:43
5:23	16:44	26:55	33:27	50:11	53:50	1:06:54	1:10:31	1:20:45	1:23:38	1:40:22	1:47:40	2:21:09
5:24	16:47	27:00	33:33	50:20	54:00	1:07:06	1:10:44	1:21:00	1:23:53	1:40:40	1:48:00	2:21:35
5:25	16:50	27:05	33:39	50:29	54:10	1:07:19	1:10:58	1:21:15	1:24:09	1:40:58	1:48:20	2:22:01
5:26	16:53	27:10	33:46	50:39	54:20	1:07:31	1:11:11	1:21:30	1:24:24	1:41:18	1:48:40	2:22:27
5:27	16:56	27:15	33:52	50:48	54:30	1:07:44	1:11:24	1:21:45	1:24:40	1:41:36	1:49:00	2:22:54
5:28	16:59	27:20	33:58	50:57	54:40	1:07:56	1:11:37	1:22:00	1:24:55	1:41:54	1:49:20	2:23:20
5:29	17:02	27:25	34:04	51:06	54:50	1:08:09	1:11:50	1:22:15	1:25:11	1:42:12	1:49:40	2:23:46
5:30	17:05	27:30	34:11	51:16	55:00	1:08:21	1:12:03	1:22:30	1:25:26	1:42:32	1:50:00	2:24:12
5:31	17:08	27:35	34:17	51:25	55:10	1:08:33	1:12:16	1:22:45	1:25:41	1:42:50	1:50:20	2:24:38
5:32	17:11	27:40	34:23	51:34	55:20	1:08:46	1:12:29	1:23:00	1:25:57	1:43:08	1:50:40	2:25:05
5:33	17:15	27:45	34:29	51:44	55:30	1:08:58	1:12:42	1:23:15	1:26:13	1:43:28	1:51:00	2:25:31
5:34	17:18	27:50	34:35	51:53	55:40	1:09:11	1:12:55	1:23:30	1:26:29	1:43:46	1:51:20	2:25:57
5:35	17:21	27:55	34:42	52:02	55:50	1:09:23	1:13:08	1:23:45	1:26:44	1:44:04	1:51:40	2:26:23
5:36	17:24	28:00	34:48	52:12	56:00	1:09:36	1:13:22	1:24:00	1:27:00	1:44:24	1:52:00	2:26:50
5:37	17:27	28:05	34:54	52:21	56:10	1:09:48	1:13:35	1:24:15	1:27:15	1:44:42	1:52:20	2:27:16
5:38	17:30	28:10	35:00	52:30	56:20	1:10:00	1:13:48	1:24:30	1:27:30	1:45:00	1:52:40	2:27:42
5:39	17:33	28:15	35:06	52:40	56:30	1:10:13	1:14:01	1:24:45	1:27:46	1:45:20	1:53:00	2:28:08
5:40	17:36	28:20	35:13	52:49	56:40	1:10:25	1:14:14	1:25:00	1:28:01	1:45:38	1:53:20	2:28:34
5:41	17:39	28:25	35:19	52:58	56:50	1:10:38	1:14:27	1:25:15	1:28:17	1:45:56	1:53:40	2:29:01
5:42	17:43	28:30	35:25	53:08	57:00	1:10:50	1:14:40	1:25:30	1:28:33	1:46:16	1:54:00	2:29:27
5:43	17:46	28:35	35:31	53:17	57:10	1:11:03	1:14:53	1:25:45	1:28:49	1:46:34	1:54:20	2:29:53

MILE TO MARATHON PACING CHART (CONT.)

MILE PACE	5K	5 MI	10K	15 K	10 MI	20K	13.1 MI	15 MI	25K	30K	20 MI	MARATHON 26.219
5:44	17:49	28:40	35:38	53:26	57:20	1:11:15	1:15:06	1:26:00	1:29:04	1:46:52	1:54:40	2:30:19
5:45	17:52	28:45	35:44	53:36	57:30	1:11:27	1:15:19	1:26:15	1:29:19	1:47:12	1:55:00	2:30:46
5:46	17:55	28:50	35:50	53:45	57:40	1:11:40	1:15:33	1:26:30	1:29:35	1:47:30	1:55:20	2:31:12
5:47	17:58	28:55	35:56	53:54	57:50	1:11:52	1:15:46	1:26:45	1:29:50	1:47:48	1:55:40	2:31:38
5:48	18:01	29:00	36:02	54:04	58:00	1:12:05	1:15:59	1:27:00	1:30:06	1:48:08	1:56:00	2:32:04
5:49	18:04	29:05	36:09	54:13	58:10	1:12:17	1:16:12	1:27:15	1:30:21	1:48:26	1:56:20	2:32:30
5:50	18:07	29:10	36:15	54:22	58:20	1:12:30	1:16:25	1:27:30	1:30:37	1:48:44	1:56:40	2:32:57
5:51	18:11	29:15	36:21	54:32	58:30	1:12:42	1:16:38	1:27:45	1:30:53	1:49:04	1:57:00	2:33:23
5:52	18:14	29:20	36:27	54:41	58:40	1:12:54	1:16:51	1:28:00	1:31:08	1:49:22	1:57:20	2:33:49
5:53	18:17	29:25	36:33	54:50	58:50	1:13:07	1:17:04	1:28:15	1:31:24	1:49:40	1:57:40	2:34:15
5:54	18:20	29:30	36:40	54:59	59:00	1:13:19	1:17:17	1:28:30	1:31:39	1:49:58	1:58:00	2:34:42
5:55	18:23	29:35	36:46	55:09	59:10	1:13:32	1:17:30	1:28:45	1:31:55	1:50:18	1:58:20	2:35:08
5:56	18:26	29:40	36:52	55:18	59:20	1:13:44	1:17:44	1:29:00	1:32:10	1:50:36	1:58:40	2:35:34
5:57	18:29	29:45	36:58	55:27	59:30	1:13:57	1:17:57	1:29:15	1:32:25	1:50:54	1:59:00	2:36:00
5:58	18:32	29:50	37:05	55:37	59:40	1:14:09	1:18:10	1:29:30	1:32:40	1:51:14	1:59:20	2:36:26
5:59	18:35	29:55	37:11	55:46	59:50	1:14:21	1:18:23	1:29:45	1:32:56	1:51:32	1:59:40	2:36:53
6:00	18:38	30:00	37:17	55:55	1:00:00	1:14:34	1:18:36	1:30:00	1:33:12	1:51:50	2:00:00	2:37:19
6:01	18:42	30:05	37:23	56:05	1:00:10	1:14:46	1:18:49	1:30:15	1:33:28	1:52:10	2:00:20	2:37:45
6:02	18:45	30:10	37:29	56:14	1:00:20	1:14:59	1:19:02	1:30:30	1:33:44	1:52:28	2:00:40	2:38:11
6:03	18:48	30:15	37:36	56:23	1:00:30	1:15:11	1:19:15	1:30:45	1:33:59	1:52:46	2:01:00	2:38:37
6:04	18:51	30:20	37:42	56:33	1:00:40	1:15:24	1:19:28	1:31:00	1:34:15	1:53:06	2:01:20	2:39:04
6:05	18:54	30:25	37:48	56:42	1:00:50	1:15:36	1:19:41	1:31:15	1:34:30	1:53:24	2:01:40	2:39:30
6:06	18:57	30:30	37:54	56:51	1:01:00	1:15:48	1:19:55	1:31:30	1:34:45	1:53:42	2:02:00	2:39:56
6:07	19:00	30:35	38:00	57:01	1:01:10	1:16:01	1:20:08	1:31:45	1:35:01	1:54:02	2:02:20	2:40:22
6:08	19:03	30:40	38:07	57:10	1:01:20	1:16:13	1:20:21	1:32:00	1:35:16	1:54:20	2:02:40	2:40:49
6:09	19:06	30:45	38:13	57:19	1:01:30	1:16:26	1:20:34	1:32:15	1:35:32	1:54:38	2:03:00	2:41:15
6:10	19:10	30:50	38:19	57:29	1:01:40	1:16:38	1:20:47	1:32:30	1:35:48	1:54:58	2:03:20	2:41:41

MILE PACE	5K	5 MI	10K	15 K	10 MI	20K	13.1 MI	15 MI	25K	30K	20 MI	MARATHON 26.219
6:11	19:13	30:55	38:25	57:38	1:01:50	1:16:51	1:21:00	1:32:45	1:36:04	1:55:16	2:03:40	2:42:07
6:12	19:16	31:00	38:32	57:47	1:02:00	1:17:03	1:21:13	1:33:00	1:36:19	1:55:34	2:04:00	2:42:33
6:13	19:19	31:05	38:38	57:57	1:02:10	1:17:15	1:21:26	1:33:15	1:36:34	1:55:58	2:04:20	2:43:00
6:14	19:22	31:10	38:44	58:06	1:02:20	1:17:28	1:21:39	1:33:30	1:36:50	1:56:12	2:04:40	2:43:26
6:15	19:25	31:15	38:50	58:15	1:02:30	1:17:40	1:21:53	1:33:45	1:37:05	1:56:30	2:05:00	2:43:52
6:16	19:28	31:20	38:56	58:25	1:02:40	1:17:53	1:22:06	1:34:00	1:37:21	1:56:50	2:05:20	2:44:18
6:17	19:31	31:25	39:03	58:34	1:02:50	1:18:05	1:22:19	1:34:15	1:37:36	1:57:08	2:05:40	2:44:45
6:18	19:34	31:30	39:09	58:43	1:03:00	1:18:18	1:22:32	1:34:30	1:37:52	1:57:26	2:06:00	2:45:11
6:19	19:37	31:35	39:15	58:52	1:03:10	1:18:30	1:22:45	1:34:45	1:38:07	1:57:44	2:06:20	2:45:37
6:20	19:41	31:40	39:21	59:02	1:03:20	1:18:42	1:22:58	1:35:00	1:38:23	1:58:04	2:06:40	2:46:03
6:21	19:44	31:45	39:27	59:11	1:03:30	1:18:55	1:23:11	1:35:15	1:38:39	1:58:22	2:07:00	2:46:29
6:22	19:47	31:50	39:34	59:20	1:03:40	1:19:07	1:23:24	1:35:30	1:38:54	1:58:40	2:07:20	2:46:56
6:23	19:50	31:55	39:40	59:30	1:03:50	1:19:20	1:23:37	1:35:45	1:39:10	1:59:00	2:07:40	2:47:22
6:24	19:53	32:00	39:46	59:39	1:04:00	1:19:32	1:23:50	1:36:00	1:39:25	1:59:18	2:08:00	2:47:48
6:25	19:56	32:05	39:52	59:48	1:04:10	1:19:45	1:24:04	1:36:15	1:39:41	1:59:36	2:08:20	2:48:14
6:26	19:59	32:10	39:58	59:58	1:04:20	1:19:57	1:24:17	1:36:30	1:39:56	1:59:56	2:08:40	2:48:41
6:27	20:02	32:15	40:05	1:00:07	1:04:30	1:20:09	1:24:30	1:36:45	1:40:11	2:00:14	2:09:00	2:49:07
6:28	20:05	32:20	40:11	1:00:16	1:04:40	1:20:22	1:24:43	1:37:00	1:40:27	2:00:32	2:09:20	2:49:33
6:29	20:09	32:25	40:17	1:00:26	1:04:50	1:20:34	1:24:56	1:37:15	1:40:43	2:00:52	2:09:40	2:49:59
6:30	20:12	32:30	40:23	1:00:35	1:05:00	1:20:47	1:25:09	1:37:30	1:40:59	2:01:10	2:10:00	2:50:25
6:31	20:15	32:35	40:30	1:00:44	1:05:10	1:20:59	1:25:22	1:37:45	1:41:14	2:01:28	2:10:20	2:50:52
6:32	20:18	32:40	40:36	1:00:54	1:05:20	1:21:12	1:25:35	1:38:00	1:41:30	2:01:48	2:10:40	2:51:18
6:33	20:21	32:45	40:42	1:01:03	1:05:30	1:21:24	1:25:48	1:38:15	1:41:45	2:02:06	2:11:00	2:51:44
6:34	20:24	32:50	40:48	1:01:12	1:05:40	1:21:36	1:26:01	1:38:30	1:42:00	2:02:24	2:11:20	2:52:10
6:35	20:27	32:55	40:54	1:01:22	1:05:50	1:21:49	1:26:15	1:38:45	1:42:16	2:02:44	2:11:40	2:52:37
6:36	20:30	33:00	41:01	1:01:31	1:06:00	1:22:01	1:26:28	1:39:00	1:42:31	2:03:02	2:12:00	2:53:03
6:37	20:33	33:05	41:07	1:01:40	1:06:10	1:22:14	1:26:41	1:39:15	1:42:47	2:03:20	2:12:20	2:53:29

MILE TO MARATHON PACING CHART (CONT.)

MILE PACE	5K	5 MI	10K	15 K	10 MI	20K	13.1 MI	15 MI	25K	30K	20 MI	MARATHON 26.219
6:38	20:37	33:10	41:13	1:01:50	1:06:20	1:22:26	1:26:54	1:39:30	1:43:03	2:03:40	2:12:40	2:53:55
6:39	20:40	33:15	41:19	1:01:59	1:06:30	1:22:39	1:27:07	1:39:45	1:43:19	2:03:58	2:13:00	2:54:21
6:40	20:43	33:20	41:25	1:02:08	1:06:40	1:22:51	1:27:20	1:40:00	1:43:34	2:04:16	2:13:20	2:54:48
6:41	20:46	33:25	41:32	1:02:18	1:06:50	1:23:03	1:27:33	1:40:15	1:43:49	2:04:36	2:13:40	2:55:14
6:42	20:49	33:30	41:38	1:02:27	1:07:00	1:23:16	1:27:46	1:40:30	1:44:05	2:04:54	2:14:00	2:55:40
6:43	20:52	33:35	41:44	1:02:36	1:07:10	1:23:28	1:27:59	1:40:45	1:44:20	2:05:12	2:14:20	2:56:06
6:44	20:55	33:40	41:50	1:02:46	1:07:20	1:23:41	1:28:12	1:41:00	1:44:36	2:05:32	2:14:40	2:56:32
6:45	20:58	33:45	41:57	1:02:55	1:07:30	1:23:53	1:28:25	1:41:15	1:44:51	2:05:50	2:15:00	2:56:59
6:46	21:01	33:50	42:03	1:03:04	1:07:40	1:24:06	1:28:39	1:41:30	1:45:07	2:06:08	2:15:20	2:57:25
6:47	21:04	33:55	42:09	1:03:13	1:07:50	1:24:18	1:28:52	1:41:45	1:45:22	2:06:26	2:15:40	2:57:51
6:48	21:08	34:00	42:15	1:03:23	1:08:00	1:24:30	1:29:05	1:42:00	1:45:38	2:06:46	2:16:00	2:58:17
6:49	21:11	34:05	42:21	1:03:32	1:08:10	1:24:43	1:29:18	1:42:15	1:45:54	2:07:04	2:16:20	2:58:44
6:50	21:14	34:10	42:28	1:03:41	1:08:20	1:24:55	1:29:31	1:42:30	1:46:09	2:07:22	2:16:40	2:59:10
6:51	21:17	34:15	42:34	1:03:51	1:08:30	1:25:08	1:29:44	1:42:45	1:46:25	2:07:42	2:17:00	2:59:36
6:52	21:20	34:20	42:40	1:04:00	1:08:40	1:25:20	1:29:57	1:43:00	1:46:40	2:08:00	2:17:20	3:00:02
6:53	21:23	34:25	42:46	1:04:09	1:08:50	1:25:33	1:30:10	1:43:15	1:46:56	2:08:18	2:17:40	3:00:28
6:54	21:26	34:30	42:52	1:04:19	1:09:00	1:25:45	1:30:23	1:43:30	1:47:11	2:08:38	2:18:00	3:00:55
6:55	21:29	34:35	42:59	1:04:28	1:09:10	1:25:57	1:30:36	1:43:45	1:47:26	2:08:56	2:18:20	3:01:21
6:56	21:32	34:40	43:05	1:04:37	1:09:20	1:26:10	1:30:50	1:44:00	1:47:42	2:09:14	2:18:40	3:01:47
6:57	21:36	34:45	43:11	1:04:47	1:09:30	1:26:22	1:31:03	1:44:15	1:47:58	2:09:34	2:19:00	3:02:13
6:58	21:39	34:50	43:17	1:04:56	1:09:40	1:26:35	1:31:16	1:44:30	1:48:14	2:09:52	2:19:20	3:02:40
6:59	21:42	34:55	43:24	1:05:05	1:09:50	1:26:47	1:31:29	1:44:45	1:48:29	2:10:10	2:19:40	3:03:06
7:00	21:45	35:00	43:30	1:05:15	1:10:00	1:27:00	1:31:42	1:45:00	1:48:45	2:10:30	2:20:00	3:03:32
7:01	21:48	35:05	43:36	1:05:24	1:10:10	1:27:12	1:31:55	1:45:15	1:49:00	2:10:48	2:20:20	3:03:58
7:02	21:51	35:10	43:42	1:05:33	1:10:20	1:27:24	1:32:08	1:45:30	1:49:15	2:11:06	2:20:40	3:04:24
7:03	21:54	35:15	43:48	1:05:43	1:10:30	1:27:37	1:32:21	1:45:45	1:49:31	2:11:26	2:21:00	3:04:51
7:04	21:57	35:20	43:55	1:05:52	1:10:40	1:27:49	1:32:34	1:46:00	1:49:46	2:11:44	2:21:20	3:05:17

MILE PACE	5K	5 MI	10K	15 K	10 MI	20K	13.1 MI	15 MI	25K	30K	20 MI	MARATHON 26.219
7:05	22:00	35:25	44:01	1:06:01	1:10:50	1:28:02	1:32:47	1:46:15	1:50:02	2:12:02	2:21:40	3:05:43
7:06	22:04	35:30	44:07	1:06:11	1:11:00	1:28:14	1:33:01	1:46:30	1:50:18	2:12:22	2:22:00	3:06:09
7:07	22:07	35:35	44:13	1:06:20	1:11:10	1:28:27	1:33:14	1:46:45	1:50:34	2:12:40	2:22:20	3:06:36
7:08	22:10	35:40	44:19	1:06:29	1:11:20	1:28:39	1:33:27	1:47:00	1:50:49	2:12:58	2:22:40	3:07:02
7:09	22:13	35:45	44:26	1:06:39	1:11:30	1:28:51	1:33:40	1:47:15	1:51:04	2:13:18	2:23:00	3:07:28
7:10	22:16	35:50	44:32	1:06:48	1:11:40	1:29:04	1:33:53	1:47:30	1:51:20	2:13:36	2:23:20	3:07:54
7:11	22:19	35:55	44:38	1:06:57	1:11:50	1:29:16	1:34:06	1:47:45	1:51:35	2:13:54	2:23:40	3:08:20
7:12	22:22	36:00	44:44	1:07:06	1:12:00	1:29:29	1:34:19	1:48:00	1:51:51	2:14:12	2:24:00	3:08:47
7:13	22:25	36:05	44:51	1:07:16	1:12:10	1:29:41	1:34:32	1:48:15	1:52:06	2:14:32	2:24:20	3:09:13
7:14	22:28	36:10	44:57	1:07:25	1:12:20	1:29:54	1:34:45	1:48:30	1:52:22	2:14:50	2:24:40	3:09:39
7:15	22:31	36:15	45:03	1:07:34	1:12:30	1:30:06	1:34:58	1:48:45	1:52:37	2:15:08	2:25:00	3:10:05
7:16	22:35	36:20	45:09	1:07:44	1:12:40	1:30:18	1:35:12	1:49:00	1:52:53	2:15:28	2:25:20	3:10:31
7:17	22:38	36:25	45:15	1:07:53	1:12:50	1:30:31	1:35:25	1:49:15	1:53:09	2:15:46	2:25:40	3:10:58
7:18	22:41	36:30	45:22	1:08:02	1:13:00	1:30:43	1:35:38	1:49:30	1:53:24	2:16:04	2:26:00	3:11:24
7:19	22:44	36:35	45:28	1:08:12	1:13:10	1:30:56	1:35:51	1:49:45	1:53:40	2:16:24	2:26:20	3:11:50
7:20	22:47	36:40	45:34	1:08:21	1:13:20	1:31:08	1:36:04	1:50:00	1:53:55	2:16:42	2:26:40	3:12:16
7:21	22:50	36:45	45:40	1:08:30	1:13:30	1:31:20	1:36:17	1:50:15	1:54:10	2:17:00	2:27:00	3:12:43
7:22	22:53	36:50	45:46	1:08:40	1:13:40	1:31:33	1:36:30	1:50:30	1:54:26	2:17:18	2:27:20	3:13:09
7:23	22:56	36:55	45:53	1:08:49	1:13:50	1:31:45	1:36:43	1:50:45	1:54:41	2:17:38	2:27:40	3:13:35
7:24	22:59	37:00	45:59	1:08:58	1:14:00	1:31:58	1:36:56	1:51:00	1:54:57	2:17:56	2:28:00	3:14:01
7:25	23:03	37:05	46:05	1:09:08	1:14:10	1:32:10	1:37:09	1:51:15	1:55:13	2:18:16	2:28:20	3:14:27
7:26	23:06	37:10	46:11	1:09:17	1:14:20	1:32:23	1:37:23	1:51:30	1:55:29	2:18:34	2:28:40	3:14:54
7:27	23:09	37:15	46:18	1:09:26	1:14:30	1:32:35	1:37:36	1:51:45	1:55:44	2:18:52	2:29:00	3:15:20
7:28	23:12	37:20	46:24	1:09:36	1:14:40	1:32:47	1:37:49	1:52:00	1:55:59	2:19:12	2:29:20	3:15:46
7:29	23:15	37:25	46:30	1:09:45	1:14:50	1:33:00	1:38:02	1:52:15	1:56:15	2:19:30	2:29:40	3:16:12
7:30	23:18	37:30	46:36	1:09:54	1:15:00	1:33:12	1:38:15	1:52:30	1:56:30	2:19:48	2:30:00	3:16:39
7:31	23:21	37:35	46:42	1:10:04	1:15:10	1:33:25	1:38:28	1:52:45	1:56:46	2:20:08	2:30:20	3:17:05

MILE TO MARATHON PACING CHART (CONT.)

MILE PACE	5K	5 MI	10K	15 K	10 MI	20K	13.1 MI	15 MI	25K	30K	20 MI	MARATHON 26.219
7:32	23:24	37:40	46:49	1:10:13	1:15:20	1:33:37	1:38:41	1:53:00	1:57:01	2:20:26	2:30:40	3:17:31
7:33	23:27	37:45	46:55	1:10:22	1:15:30	1:33:50	1:38:54	1:53:15	1:57:17	2:20:44	2:31:00	3:17:57
7:34	23:31	37:50	47:01	1:10:32	1:15:40	1:34:02	1:39:07	1:53:30	1:57:33	2:21:04	2:31:20	3:18:23
7:35	23:34	37:55	47:07	1:10:41	1:15:50	1:34:14	1:39:21	1:53:45	1:57:48	2:21:22	2:31:40	3:18:50
7:36	23:37	38:00	47:13	1:10:50	1:16:00	1:34:27	1:39:34	1:54:00	1:58:04	2:21:40	2:32:00	3:19:16
7:37	23:40	38:05	47:20	1:10:59	1:16:10	1:34:39	1:39:47	1:54:15	1:58:19	2:21:58	2:32:20	3:19:42
7:38	23:43	38:10	47:26	1:11:09	1:16:20	1:34:52	1:40:00	1:54:30	1:58:35	2:22:18	2:32:40	3:20:09
7:39	23:46	38:15	47:32	1:11:18	1:16:30	1:35:04	1:40:13	1:54:45	1:58:50	2:22:36	2:33:00	3:20:35
7:40	23:49	38:20	47:38	1:11:27	1:16:40	1:35:17	1:40:26	1:55:00	1:59:06	2:22:54	2:33:20	3:21:01
7:41	23:52	38:25	47:45	1:11:37	1:16:50	1:35:29	1:40:39	1:55:15	1:59:21	2:23:14	2:33:40	3:21:27
7:42	23:55	38:30	47:51	1:11:46	1:17:00	1:35:41	1:40:52	1:55:30	1:59:36	2:23:32	2:34:00	3:21:53
7:43	23:58	38:35	47:57	1:11:55	1:17:10	1:35:54	1:41:05	1:55:45	1:59:52	2:23:50	2:34:20	3:22:19
7:44	24:02	38:40	48:03	1:12:05	1:17:20	1:36:06	1:41:18	1:56:00	2:00:08	2:24:10	2:34:40	3:22:46
7:45	24:05	38:45	48:09	1:12:14	1:17:30	1:36:19	1:41:32	1:56:15	2:00:24	2:24:28	2:35:00	3:23:12
7:46	24:08	38:50	48:16	1:12:23	1:17:40	1:36:31	1:41:45	1:56:30	2:00:39	2:24:46	2:35:20	3:23:38
7:47	24:11	38:55	48:22	1:12:33	1:17:50	1:36:44	1:41:58	1:56:45	2:00:55	2:25:06	2:35:40	3:24:04
7:48	24:14	39:00	48:28	1:12:42	1:18:00	1:36:56	1:42:11	1:57:00	2:01:10	2:25:24	2:36:00	3:24:30
7:49	24:17	39:05	48:34	1:12:51	1:18:10	1:37:08	1:42:24	1:57:15	2:01:25	2:25:42	2:36:20	3:24:57
7:50	24:20	39:10	48:40	1:13:01	1:18:20	1:37:21	1:42:37	1:57:30	2:01:41	2:26:02	2:36:40	3:25:23
7:51	24:23	39:15	48:47	1:13:10	1:18:30	1:37:33	1:42:50	1:57:45	2:01:56	2:26:20	2:37:00	3:25:49
7:52	24:26	39:20	48:53	1:13:19	1:18:40	1:37:46	1:43:03	1:58:00	2:02:12	2:26:38	2:37:20	3:26:15
7:53	24:30	39:25	48:59	1:13:29	1:18:50	1:37:58	1:43:16	1:58:15	2:02:28	2:26:58	2:37:40	3:26:42
7:54	24:33	39:30	49:05	1:13:38	1:19:00	1:38:11	1:43:29	1:58:30	2:02:44	2:27:16	2:38:00	3:27:08
7:55	24:36	39:35	49:12	1:13:47	1:19:10	1:38:23	1:43:43	1:58:45	2:02:59	2:27:34	2:38:20	3:27:34
7:56	24:39	39:40	49:18	1:13:57	1:19:20	1:38:35	1:43:56	1:59:00	2:03:14	2:27:54	2:38:40	3:28:00
7:57	24:42	39:45	49:24	1:14:06	1:19:30	1:38:48	1:44:09	1:59:15	2:03:30	2:28:12	2:39:00	3:28:26
7:58	24:45	39:50	49:30	1:14:15	1:19:40	1:39:00	1:44:22	1:59:30	2:03:45	2:28:30	2:39:20	3:28:53

MILE PACE	5K	5 MI	10K	15 K	10 MI	20K	13.1 MI	15 MI	25K	30K	20 MI	MARATHON 26.219
7:59	24:48	39:55	49:36	1:14:25	1:19:50	1:39:13	1:44:35	1:59:45	2:04:01	2:28:50	2:39:40	3:29:19
8:00	24:51	40:00	49:43	1:14:34	1:20:00	1:39:25	1:44:48	2:00:00	2:04:16	2:29:06	2:40:00	3:29:45
8:01	24:54	40:05	49:49	1:14:43	1:20:10	1:39:38	1:45:01	2:00:15	2:04:32	2:29:26	2:40:20	3:30:11
8:02	24:58	40:10	49:55	1:14:53	1:20:20	1:39:50	1:45:14	2:00:30	2:04:48	2:29:46	2:40:40	3:30:38
8:03	25:01	40:15	50:01	1:15:02	1:20:30	1:40:02	1:45:27	2:00:45	2:05:03	2:30:04	2:41:00	3:31:04
8:04	25:04	40:20	50:07	1:15:11	1:20:40	1:40:15	1:45:40	2:01:00	2:05:19	2:30:22	2:41:20	3:31:30
8:05	25:07	40:25	50:14	1:15:20	1:20:50	1:40:27	1:45:53	2:01:15	2:05:34	2:30:40	2:41:40	3:31:56
8:06	25:10	40:30	50:20	1:15:30	1:21:00	1:40:40	1:46:07	2:01:30	2:05:50	2:31:00	2:42:00	3:32:22
8:07	25:13	40:35	50:26	1:15:39	1:21:10	1:40:52	1:46:20	2:01:45	2:06:06	2:31:18	2:42:20	3:32:49
8:08	25:16	40:40	50:32	1:15:48	1:21:20	1:41:05	1:46:33	2:02:00	2:06:21	2:31:36	2:42:40	3:33:15
8:09	25:19	40:45	50:39	1:15:58	1:21:30	1:41:17	1:46:46	2:02:15	2:06:36	2:31:56	2:43:00	3:33:41
8:10	25:22	40:50	50:45	1:16:07	1:21:40	1:41:29	1:46:59	2:02:30	2:06:51	2:32:14	2:43:20	3:34:07
8:11	25:25	40:55	50:51	1:16:16	1:21:50	1:41:42	1:47:12	2:02:45	2:07:07	2:32:32	2:43:40	3:34:34
8:12	25:29	41:00	50:57	1:16:26	1:22:00	1:41:54	1:47:25	2:03:00	2:07:23	2:32:52	2:44:00	3:35:00
8:13	25:32	41:05	51:03	1:16:35	1:22:10	1:42:07	1:47:38	2:03:15	2:07:39	2:33:10	2:44:20	3:35:26
8:14	25:35	41:10	51:10	1:16:44	1:22:20	1:42:19	1:47:51	2:03:30	2:07:54	2:33:28	2:44:40	3:35:52
8:15	25:38	41:15	51:16	1:16:54	1:22:30	1:42:32	1:48:04	2:03:45	2:08:10	2:33:48	2:45:00	3:36:18
8:16	25:41	41:20	51:22	1:17:03	1:22:40	1:42:44	1:48:18	2:04:00	2:08:25	2:34:06	2:45:20	3:36:45
8:17	25:44	41:25	51:28	1:17:12	1:22:50	1:42:56	1:48:31	2:04:15	2:08:40	2:34:24	2:45:40	3:37:11
8:18	25:47	41:30	51:34	1:17:22	1:23:00	1:43:09	1:48:44	2:04:30	2:08:56	2:34:44	2:46:00	3:37:37
8:19	25:50	41:35	51:41	1:17:31	1:23:10	1:43:21	1:48:57	2:04:45	2:09:11	2:35:02	2:46:20	3:38:03
8:20	25:53	41:40	51:47	1:17:40	1:23:20	1:43:34	1:49:10	2:05:00	2:09:27	2:35:20	2:46:40	3:38:29
8:21	25:57	41:45	51:53	1:17:50	1:23:30	1:43:46	1:49:23	2:05:15	2:09:43	2:35:40	2:47:00	3:38:56
8:22	26:00	41:50	51:59	1:17:59	1:23:40	1:43:59	1:49:36	2:05:30	2:09:59	2:35:58	2:47:20	3:39:22
8:23	26:03	41:55	52:05	1:18:08	1:23:50	1:44:11	1:49:49	2:05:45	2:10:14	2:36:16	2:47:40	3:39:48
8:24	26:06	42:00	52:12	1:18:18	1:24:00	1:44:23	1:50:02	2:06:00	2:10:29	2:36:36	2:48:00	3:40:14
8:25	26:09	42:05	52:18	1:18:27	1:24:10	1:44:36	1:50:15	2:06:15	2:10:45	2:36:54	2:48:20	3:40:41

MILE TO MARATHON PACING CHART (CONT.)

MILE PACE	5K	5 MI	10K	15 K	10 MI	20K	13.1 MI	15 MI	25K	30K	20 MI	MARATHON 26.219
8:26	26:12	42:10	52:24	1:18:36	1:24:20	1:44:48	1:50:29	2:06:30	2:11:00	2:37:12	2:48:40	3:41:07
8:27	26:15	42:15	52:30	1:18:46	1:24:30	1:45:01	1:50:42	2:06:45	2:11:16	2:37:32	2:49:00	3:41:33
8:28	26:18	42:20	52:37	1:18:55	1:24:40	1:45:13	1:50:55	2:07:00	2:11:31	2:37:50	2:49:20	3:41:59
8:29	26:21	42:25	52:43	1:19:04	1:24:50	1:45:26	1:51:08	2:07:15	2:11:47	2:38:08	2:49:40	3:42:25
8:30	26:24	42:30	52:49	1:19:13	1:25:00	1:45:38	1:51:21	2:07:30	2:12:02	2:38:26	2:50:00	3:42:52
8:31	26:28	42:35	52:55	1:19:23	1:25:10	1:45:50	1:51:34	2:07:45	2:12:18	2:38:46	2:50:20	3:43:18
8:32	26:31	42:40	53:01	1:19:32	1:25:20	1:46:03	1:51:47	2:08:00	2:12:34	2:39:04	2:50:40	3:43:44
8:33	26:34	42:45	53:08	1:19:41	1:25:30	1:46:15	1:52:00	2:08:15	2:12:49	2:39:22	2:51:00	3:44:10
8:34	26:37	42:50	53:14	1:19:51	1:25:40	1:46:28	1:52:13	2:08:30	2:13:05	2:39:42	2:51:20	3:44:37
8:35	26:40	42:55	53:20	1:20:00	1:25:50	1:46:40	1:52:26	2:08:45	2:13:20	2:40:00	2:51:40	3:45:03
8:36	26:43	43:00	53:26	1:20:09	1:26:00	1:46:53	1:52:40	2:09:00	2:13:36	2:40:18	2:52:00	3:45:29
8:37	26:46	43:05	53:32	1:20:19	1:26:10	1:47:05	1:52:53	2:09:15	2:13:51	2:40:38	2:52:20	3:45:55
8:38	26:49	43:10	53:39	1:20:28	1:26:20	1:47:17	1:53:06	2:09:30	2:14:06	2:40:56	2:52:40	3:46:21
8:39	26:52	43:15	53:45	1:20:37	1:26:30	1:47:30	1:53:19	2:09:45	2:14:22	2:41:14	2:53:00	3:46:48
8:40	26:56	43:20	53:51	1:20:47	1:26:40	1:47:42	1:53:32	2:10:00	2:14:38	2:41:34	2:53:20	3:47:14
8:41	26:59	43:25	53:57	1:20:56	1:26:50	1:47:55	1:53:45	2:10:15	2:14:54	2:41:52	2:53:40	3:47:40
8:42	27:02	43:30	54:04	1:21:05	1:27:00	1:48:07	1:53:58	2:10:30	2:15:09	2:42:10	2:54:00	3:48:06
8:43	27:05	43:35	54:10	1:21:15	1:27:10	1:48:20	1:54:11	2:10:45	2:15:25	2:42:30	2:54:20	3:48:33
8:44	27:08	43:40	54:16	1:21:24	1:27:20	1:48:32	1:54:24	2:11:00	2:15:40	2:42:48	2:54:40	3:48:59
8:45	27:11	43:45	54:22	1:21:33	1:27:30	1:48:44	1:54:38	2:11:15	2:15:55	2:43:06	2:55:00	3:49:25
8:46	27:14	43:50	54:28	1:21:43	1:27:40	1:48:57	1:54:51	2:11:30	2:16:11	2:43:26	2:55:20	3:49:51
8:47	27:17	43:55	54:35	1:21:52	1:27:50	1:49:09	1:55:04	2:11:45	2:16:26	2:43:44	2:55:40	3:50:17
8:48	27:20	44:00	54:41	1:22:01	1:28:00	1:49:22	1:55:17	2:12:00	2:16:42	2:44:02	2:56:00	3:50:44
8:49	27:24	44:05	54:47	1:22:11	1:28:10	1:49:34	1:55:30	2:12:15	2:16:58	2:44:22	2:56:20	3:51:10
8:50	27:27	44:10	54:53	1:22:20	1:28:20	1:49:47	1:55:43	2:12:30	2:17:14	2:44:40	2:56:40	3:51:36
8:51	27:30	44:15	54:59	1:22:29	1:28:30	1:49:59	1:55:56	2:12:45	2:17:29	2:44:48	2:57:00	3:52:02
8:52	27:33	44:20	55:06	1:22:39	1:28:40	1:50:11	1:56:09	2:13:00	2:17:44	2:45:18	2:57:20	3:52:29

MILE PACE	5K	5 MI	10K	15 K	10 MI	20K	13.1 MI	15 MI	25K	30K	20 MI	MARATHON 26.219
8:53	27:36	44:25	55:12	1:22:48	1:28:50	1:50:24	1:56:22	2:13:15	2:18:00	2:45:36	2:57:40	3:52:55
8:54	27:39	44:30	55:18	1:22:57	1:29:00	1:50:36	1:56:35	2:13:30	2:18:15	2:45:54	2:58:00	3:53:21
8:55	27:42	44:35	55:24	1:23:07	1:29:10	1:50:49	1:56:49	2:13:45	2:18:31	2:46:14	2:58:20	3:53:47
8:56	27:45	44:40	55:31	1:23:16	1:29:20	1:51:01	1:57:02	2:14:00	2:18:46	2:46:32	2:58:40	3:54:13
8:57	27:48	44:45	55:37	1:23:25	1:29:30	1:51:14	1:57:15	2:14:15	2:19:02	2:46:50	2:59:00	3:54:40
8:58	27:51	44:50	55:43	1:23:34	1:29:40	1:51:26	1:57:28	2:14:30	2:19:17	2:47:08	2:59:20	3:55:06
8:59	27:55	44:55	55:49	1:23:44	1:29:50	1:51:38	1:57:41	2:14:45	2:19:36	2:47:28	2:59:40	3:55:32
9:00	27:58	45:00	55:55	1:23:53	1:30:00	1:51:51	1:57:54	2:15:00	2:19:58	2:47:46	3:00:00	3:55:58
9:10	28:29	45:50	56:58	1:25:27	1:31:40	1:53:56	2:00:11	2:17:30	2:22:25	2:50:54	3:03:20	4:00:22
9:20	29:00	46:40	58:00	1:27:00	1:33:20	1:56:00	2:02:22	2:20:00	2:25:00	2:54:00	3:06:40	4:04:44
9:30	29:31	47:30	59:02	1:28:33	1:35:00	1:58:04	2:04:33	2:22:30	2:27:35	2:57:06	3:10:00	4:09:06
9:40	30:02	48:20	60:05	1:30:07	1:36:40	2:00:10	2:06:44	2:25:00	2:30:12	3:00:15	3:13:20	4:13:28
9:50	30:33	49:10	61:07	1:31:40	1:38:20	2:02:14	2:08:55	2:27:30	2:32:47	3:03:21	3:16:40	4:17:50
10:00	31:05	50:00	62:09	1:33:14	1:40:00	2:04:18	2:11:07	2:30:00	2:35:23	3:06:27	3:20:00	4:22:13

MILE/KILOMETER TIME COMPARISONS

Mile	Kilometer	Mile	Kilometer
4:00	2:29.16	7:00	4:21.03
4:10	2:35.37	7:10	4:27.24
4:20	2:41.59	7:20	4:33.46
4:30	2:47.80	7:30	4:39.67
4:40	2:54.02	7:40	4:45.89
4:50	3:00.23	7:50	4:52.10
5:00	3:06.45	8:00	4:58.32
5:10	3:12.66	8:10	5:04.53
5:20	3:18.88	8:20	5:10.75
5:30	3:25.09	8:30	5:16.96
5:40	3:31.31	8:40	5:23.18
5:50	3:37.52	8:50	5:29.39
6:00	3:43.74	9:00	5:35.61
6:10	3:49.95	9:10	5:41.82
6:20	3:56.17	9:20	5:48.04
6:30	4:02.38	9:30	5:54.25
6:40	4:08.60	9:40	6:00.47
6:50	4:14.81	9:50	6:06.68

1-HOUR-RUN PACING CHART

Distance	Per Mile	Distance	Per Mile	Distance	Per Mile	Distance	Per Mile
6 miles	10:00.00	8 miles	7:30.00	10 miles	6:00.00	12 miles	5:00.00
6¼ miles	9:36.00	8¼ miles	7:16.32	10¼ miles	5:51.24	12¼ miles	4:53.88
6½ miles	9:13.32	8½ miles	7:03.44	10½ miles	5:42.84	12½ miles	4:48.00
6¾ miles	8:53.28	8¾ miles	6:51.42	10¾ miles	5:34.80	12¾ miles	4:42.36
7 miles	8:35.46	9 miles	6:40.00	11 miles	5:27.24	13 miles	4:36.90
7¼ miles	8:16.50	9¼ miles	6:29.16	11¼ miles	5:20.00		
7½ miles	8:00.00	9½ miles	6:19.02	11½ miles	5:13.08		
7¾ miles	7:44.50	9¾ miles	6:09.24	11¾ miles	5:06.20		

CONVERTING HAND TIMES
TO ELECTRONIC TIMES

A hand time is any time recorded by a person at the finish line who actually starts and stops a watch. A fully automatic (electronic) time is recorded by a machine attached to the starter's gun, which provides a photo of the finish from which times may be read.

The International Amateur Athletic Federation (IAAF) uses the following conversions from hand times to fully automatic (electronic) times:

For all events where the start and finish are in the same place (adjacent to the actual finish line), add .14 seconds.

For all events where the start is a long distance from the finish (at the other end of the straightaway or across the infield), add .24 seconds.

An electronic time is listed to one hundreth of a second. Hand times must be rounded up to the nearest tenth. Times run in road races must be rounded up to the nearest whole second.